TABLE SETTINGS

TABLE SETTINGS

A Play by James Lapine

NELSON DOUBLEDAY, INC.
Garden City, New York

© Copyright 1980 by James Lapine
All Rights Reserved

Manufactured in the United States of America

For My Parents

Table Settings was first presented in workshop at Playwrights Horizons, New York City, in March 1979. It was directed by the author; the scenery was by Richard Goodwin; costumes by Robert Wojewodski; lighting by Annie Wrightson; sound by Michael Spellman; stage managed by Kevin Mangan. The Managing Director was Robert Moss, and the Artistic Director was Andre Bishop. The cast in order of appearance was as follows:

YOUNGER SON	*David Marshall Grant*
OLDER SON	*Clayton Berry*
WIFE	*Chris Weatherhead*
GRANDDAUGHTER	*Marta Kober*
MOTHER	*Frances Chaney*
GRANDSON	*Carlo Imperato*
GIRL FRIEND	*Carolyn Hurlburt*
VOICE OVER	*Paul Sparer*

Table Settings was first presented commercially by Stephen Graham, Luis Sanjurjo, and Joan Stein on the mainstage at Playwrights Horizons, New York City, on January 14, 1980. It was directed by the author; the scenery was by Heidi Landesman; costumes by Robert Wojewodski; lighting by Beverly Emmons; sound and stage managed by Michael Spellman. The cast in order of appearance was as follows:

YOUNGER SON	*Mark Blum*
OLDER SON	*Brent Spiner*
WIFE	*Chris Weatherhead*
GRANDDAUGHTER	*Marta Kober*

MOTHER	*Frances Chaney*
GRANDSON	*Eric Gurry*
GIRL FRIEND	*Carolyn Hurlburt*
VOICE OVER	*Paul Sparer*

TABLE SETTINGS

THE CHARACTERS

A Jewish MOTHER, proudly from Minsk, late sixties

Her OLDER SON, a divorce lawyer, mid-thirties
His WIFE, the ultimate shiksa, mid-thirties
Their daughter (GRANDDAUGHTER), a cheerleader, fourteen or bust
Their son (GRANDSON) pre-puberty and pre-Bar Mitzvah, twelve

Her YOUNGER SON, a mess, late twenties
His GIRL FRIEND, a psychiatric social worker, late twenties

A bare table stands on the stage, two end chairs at either side. As the audience enters the theater there is music playing, perhaps a radio, and work lights on the stage. A man (Younger Son) periodically appears setting the table one piece at a time. At first he is dressed in sloppy jeans, a knit cap, T-shirt, sneakers, etc. Every time he exits for another table item he returns dressed in one item of a waiter's outfit. The jeans are replaced by black pants, the T-shirt by a white shirt, the sneakers by a pair of black shoes, etc. The cap is the last item to go. By curtain time, he is wearing a complete waiter's outfit: black bow tie, red jacket, neatly combed hair. The table is completely set for two and he carries menus and places a candle at the center of the table. He lights the candle, the lights dim as we hear a radio scan which settles on some suitable restaurant music.

VOICE OVER: "TABLE SETTINGS"

A couple enters from one side. She (Wife) is wearing a kelly green dress and open-toed white sandals. He (Older Son) is wearing a three-piece suit which he has worn for years. They go to the table. Older Son thoughtlessly pulls out Wife's chair and then goes to the other side and sits down. Wife stands, annoyed that her husband has not seated her like a gentleman. Younger Son suddenly pushes the chair under her. Startled, she sits.

Younger Son flips the menu open for her. He goes to the other side of the table and hands the Older Son his menu. Older Son whispers in his ear ordering their drinks. Younger Son exits and no sooner returns with the drink order. He serves the drinks. Older Son dives into his martini immediately. Wife has her drink poised for a toast. She is hurt. Older Son realizes his mistake. He clinks his glass against hers.

A young girl (Granddaughter) enters. She is wearing a cheer-leading outfit and smoking a cigarette. She begins to walk around the table. She blows smoke in the face of the Older Son. He is oblivious. She moves around the table to the front and does a cheering jump. She exits with a giggle.

The Wife calls the waiter over and whispers into his ear. Younger Son points to the ladies room. Wife gets up, pats her nose to indicate she's going out for a powder, and exits.

Older Son reaches for another cigarette. The pack is empty. The Younger Son comes over and points offstage to the cigarette machine. The Older Son exits. The Younger Son takes the empty cigarette pack, the menus, and the glasses off the table and begins to exit.

There is the sound of another radio scan. The restaurant music switches to Cole Porter's "Just One of Those Things" or the like. A woman (Mother) enters carrying a chair which she places at the upstage center of the table. She goes to one side and pulls a leaf out from the table. She bops and swings to the other side and does the same. She exclaims:

MOTHER: Food is my passion! Food is my expression!

(She blows out the candle, lights bump up, music fades out. She speaks to the audience.)

You can't live without food, so why shouldn't I enjoy giving? Oi, there was a time when a person could take pride in setting a nice table.

(*She goes to the hutch and brings out a piece of cake and a napkin which she sets on the table.*)

In Minsk, you were respected for being a good cook, a good *balabusta*. Ech, today it's woman's lib! What do you think? I should burn my bra? I should maybe go back to school and get some cockamamie degree? I should feel guilty that I'm only a wonderful mother?

(*During the last part of her speech, around "Woman's lib!," the Wife returns from the ladies room. She can't find her husband. She looks and sees the Mother. Her one evening out has been ruined. The Older Son has returned at the same moment. He carries a full pack of cigarettes. He cannot find his table. He sees the Wife. Their eyes meet. They stare at the Mother. They approach her. As she finishes her last line, the Older Son grabs her from behind as the Wife pulls the napkin from her hands and puts it over her mouth. Younger Son has returned dressed in his cap and sloppy outfit. He smiles and holds the door open as the Mother is dragged out.*

The Younger Son sits at the table and begins eating the cake. The lights focus on the white tablecloth. The Grandson suddenly darts his head out from under the table.)

GRANDSON (*to the audience*): No one can come in here. This is my room. This is my world. No one can come in here. (*pause*) I know you want to come in here. No one can stand being kept out of anything. Everyone always wants to be everywhere. (*pause*) Well, if you really want to come in here, I suppose you can, but you know you're not supposed to.

(*He goes back under. Lights fade on him and come up on the Younger Son.*)

YOUNGER SON (*to the audience*): I used to go under there too. Now it's his turn. I can't stand confined places anymore. I can't stand the feeling that everything is so close around me. I don't know what it is. Maybe it's because I used to hide under the table. Maybe it was too many Fruit Loops for breakfast.

GIRL FRIEND (*She enters across the room.*):

You spend too much time thinking, that's your problem. I love you.

YOUNGER SON: How do you know?

GIRL FRIEND (*like speaking to a child*): I know. I can tell.

(*Moves over to him.*)

You don't connect with your feelings. You are too cerebral. And at your age. You're afraid of sex. You're afraid to break from the maternal tie. I can take you out of yourself. I can take you to small and confining rooms where you can feel free and unafraid. I can help you let go.

YOUNGER SON: I don't want to let go.

GIRL FRIEND: Now you know you don't believe that.

(*She gives him a long and seductive kiss. Mother enters from the side and watches in amazement. Girl Friend then grabs Younger Son and pulls him under the table.*)

MOTHER (*General lights up.*):

I'm an old-fashioned girl! What do you think? I like being made into a cultural stereotype?

(*She clears the table as she speaks.*)

You think I like being the topic of conversation at psychiatrists' offices? They've got their nerve. They monkey around with shiksas, and they blame me. It's my fault. I don't feel guilty! There I said it. I only wanted the best for them.

(*She is by the side of the table. Grandson, Younger Son, and Girl Friend pop their heads out from under the table.*)

Don't you look at me like that! I gave you everything and this is how you repay me?

YOUNGER SON: Oh, Mom . . .

MOTHER: Okay, I'm not bitter. I'm not angry.

(*The three of them begin to exit.*)

So, at least stay and have a little something to eat.

GIRL FRIEND: Thanks very much, but I've lost my appetite. (*She exits.*)

YOUNGER SON: Thanks, Mom, but I really am stuffed. (*He exits.*)

GRANDSON (*Pulls M&M's out of his pocket.*):

Thanks, Gram, but this is quite enough.

(*They all exit.*)

MOTHER (*Dashing after them.*):

The ice box is full and nobody's eating! (*to audience again*) So maybe I am a cultural stereotype. Listen, I never picked my personality from a sociology book. *Nisht Gefidelt!** I'm happy. I'm happy making chicken soup, playing maj on Wednesday, telling the butcher "cut it lean." If it weren't for some smart-tushy psychiatrist, I wouldn't have to apologize every time I offered a piece of sponge cake. Ech, things used to be so simple. Now you have to worry all the time you're stepping on somebody's toes.

(*She exits; the Younger Son enters from the other side.*)

* Yiddish for "It doesn't bother me."

VOICE OVER: "THE YOUNGER SON AWAKENS"

YOUNGER SON (*He staggers in carrying a dope pipe and climbs on top of the table to deliver his oration.*):

I try to let it all hang out. I try to open myself up to the world. I try to let every thought be exposed to even the most remote person. Then I get embarrassed. Then I get paranoid. It's already been said a million times on "Meet the Press," on "As the World Turns," on the last half hour of the "Merv Griffin Show." I don't want to be an asshole like everybody else.

(*He lights the pipe and takes a huge hit.*)

They say no two kidneys are alike. Every fingerprint is unique. I don't believe it for a minute. Oh, sure, one has the clothes. The hairstyle. The language of speech. The way the tongue presses against the mouth to say the words? The way the lungs expand and contract? No. It's impossible.

(*He jumps from the table.*)

After all, everyone is living a different reality. If only someone could see the world as I do. Well, maybe I'll try to get into it. Try to shut the mind off long enough to enjoy.

(*Sits at the table.*)

Maybe I'll try to get hold of some poppers. Better yet, some lithium chloride.

(*He drops his head and collapses on the table.*)

VOICE OVER: "SETTING IT ALL UP"

WIFE (*Enters carrying a chair and notices Younger Son catatonic at the table.*):

Oh, hi, kiddo, what you up to? Hey, all tuckered out again?

(*After no response she begins to set the table around him, and continues to do so throughout the scene.*)

Say, I've been meaning to tell you, I know this lovely girl. Alice's sister. She was married, but just for a short time. A career woman. Darling-looking gal. A great sense of humor. I think the two of you just might hit it off.

(*She picks his head up and sets a place under it.*)

Maybe the four of us could go to a movie and then we'll take you out to dinner.

(*Pause. Still no response.*)

Think about it. I'll get you her number.

YOUNGER SON: Are you going to do this again?

WIFE: She's a social worker. A psychiatric social worker.

YOUNGER SON (*He finally lifts his head.*):

Can she write prescriptions?

WIFE (*nervous*): Maybe she's not your type after all. Honey, we're all so worried about you. We only want you to be happy. You're so distant.

(*He takes a popper bottle from his pocket and begins to snort it. She is oblivious.*)

I know I'm not even a blood relative to be saying these things to you, but it's troubling your mother, and your brother. Even the kids seem to sense your unhappiness.

(*He reels from the poppers. She cannot ignore the gesture.*)

Oh honey, do you have a cold?

YOUNGER SON (*stoned*): Uh huh.

WIFE: What's that you're taking for it?

YOUNGER SON: Drugs.

WIFE (*stunned*): Medication?

YOUNGER SON (*with a smile*): Drugs.

WIFE: Well, if there's anything we can do.

(*He starts to get up to leave and stumbles to the door. She follows him to the exit.*)

I know how difficult life can be. (*sincere*) We love you very much. We really do. All of us.

YOUNGER SON: Can I pick the movie?

WIFE: Sure.

YOUNGER SON (*deep breath*): Okay, what's her number?

WIFE: I'll take care of everything.

YOUNGER SON: Thanks. I'm sure you will.

(*He exits.*)

VOICE OVER: "FLANKEN"

MOTHER (*Entering with a bowl and spoon which she stirs as she speaks.*):
Helen's so upset. Her son's marrying a gentile girl.

WIFE: I know.

MOTHER: Well, you feel safer with your own kind.

WIFE: I know.

MOTHER: Cultural consistency.

WIFE (*They sit at the table. The Wife files her nails as the Mother stirs.*):
I'm tired of being pigeonholed as the "WASP," the "shiksa."

MOTHER: Honey, I'm tired of being a Jewish mother.

WIFE: We were told a Jewish man was a good catch. They're more faithful. They eat before they drink. Your son drinks before he eats.

MOTHER: Takes after his father, may he rest in peace.

WIFE: Cultural consistency.

MOTHER: So, what's going to be with your brother-in-law?

WIFE: Oh, I forgot to tell you. I'm fixing him up with Alice's sister. She's Jewish. Who knows, maybe they'll even get married!

MOTHER: From your lips to God's ears.

WIFE: Huh?

MOTHER (*Pinching her on the cheek.*):
You're such a happy girl.

WIFE: Very. No one else is, but I am.

MOTHER: You shiksas don't worry so much.

WIFE: You're pigeonholing me again.

MOTHER: Sweetheart, I'm sorry. If anyone should be careful, it's me.

WIFE: Well, we shiksas have thick skin.

MOTHER: It's all those cloth coats and little open-toed sandals in the dead of winter. In Minsk you had to dress warm!

(*Pats her rather hard on the cheek.*)

I made a flanken for dinner!

(*She exits.*)

WIFE (*wincing*): Oooh, my favorite. Flanken.

VOICE OVER: "HOW WAS YOUR DAY?"

Mother, Older Son, and Younger Son enter, joining Wife at the table. Granddaughter and Grandson enter downstage carrying their own chairs.

OLDER SON: How was your day?

TOGETHER (*except Older Son*): Okay. (*They chuckle at the inadvertent collective response.*)

(*Pause.*)

MOTHER: It was so beautiful out, I hated being inside.

TOGETHER (*except Mother*): I know what you mean. (*A little less amused.*)

(*Pause.*)

GRANDSON and GRANDDAUGHTER (*They reach at the same time, smacking each other's hands.*):

Pass the butter, please.

(*Wife and Older Son make scolding noises.*)

(*Pause.*)

(*The following lines are delivered almost simultaneously.*)

OLDER SON: I had the most unbelievable divorce case today.

WIFE: There was the most wonderful woman in my yoga class today.

YOUNGER SON: I actually went for three job interviews today.

MOTHER: The butcher and I had such a terrible fight today.

GRANDDAUGHTER: Stephen Franklin attacked me at the bus stop today.

GRANDSON: There's going to be a terrific television show on to-night.

TOGETHER: That's nice. (*Not amused.*)

(*Pause.*)

(*Again almost simultaneously with some urgency.*)

MOTHER: He trimmed as much meat as fat from the brisket.

OLDER SON: This woman's husband is as queer as a three-dollar bill.

GRANDDAUGHTER: He tried to put his hand down my blouse and touch me.

WIFE: She was an operative with the Central Intelligence Agency.

YOUNGER SON: I think I might take a job as a waiter.

GRANDSON: It's all about how damaging television can be for kids.

TOGETHER: Oh, really. (*Annoyed.*)

GRANDSON and GRANDDAUGHTER: May we please be excused from the table?

WIFE and OLDER SON: Yes, you may. (*Children exit with chairs, then return and help clear table.*)

WIFE and MOTHER: Let's clear the dishes from the table. (*They clear and exit.*)

OLDER SON: I think I'll just make myself a little martini. Anything for you?

YOUNGER SON (*He is staring off into space. Older Son snaps his fingers.*):

No, thanks.

(*Older Son exits.*)

VOICE OVER: "ALICE'S SISTER"

Younger Son remains on stage.

ALICE'S SISTER: Hi, I'm Alice's sister. You know Alice, she was the most popular girl in the class; me, I had naturally curly hair and glasses. Alice was queen of the senior prom; I was president of the Kafka Club. Alice went on to college and got her MRS degree. A doctor, no less. Shortly thereafter, two perfect children; natural childbirth, of course. I think they were born toilet trained. Do you have any idea what living in the shadow of an older sister can do to a person? Any psychologist will tell you that sibling rivalry can encourage anti-social behavior. And it's a simple fact: the first born lives out the expectations of the parents and the youngest rebels. I became a lot happier when I realized: an Alice I will never be. Suddenly curly hair was fashionable, soft contacts were comfortable, excess weight was expendable. I used to feel very unattractive. I used to be a very self-destructive person. Then I began my career as a psychiatric social worker. I used to spend so much time screwing up my life —now I get paid to help other people screw up theirs.

(*She exits.*)

VOICE OVER: "NIGHTWALK"

Blackout. Mother enters the darkened room in a nightgown and carrying a candle and delivers her address around the Younger Son. There is electronic music in the background.

MOTHER (*Sleepwalking.*):

Little boy, little boy, I love you, I love you, I love you. You can do no wrong, you can do no wrong. You think it was easy coming from Minsk? You think it was easy? Oh, you in your split levels and your bachelor pads. In your deepest dreams, not in your darkest and deepest dreams do you know what it was like. Food. You think there was an abundance of food? You think one worried about food? You better believe one worried about food. All right, I'm sorry. I'm always sorry. I also hurt and feel pain. You think I don't know. You never think or believe. The years cannot wipe away the feeling of that hunger. The years cannot take that fear away.

(*She blows out the candle and exits with Younger Son in the blackout.*)

VOICE OVER: "THE GRANDSON'S TURN"

GRANDSON (*Coming from underneath the table sliding along the floor until he kneels to address the audience.*):

They want me to go to Hebrew school. Hebrew school? I can barely read English. Grandma says (*gives himself a hard pinch to the cheek*), "Sweetheart, you will be well compensated if you have a Bar Mitzvah." But I heard Mom say on the phone that she hasn't gotten over the bris yet. Do you know what a bris is?

(*He makes a cutting motion with his fingers at his crotch and then falls crying in pain.*)

I thought this religion made you do some pretty weird things until I saw a picture book on the puberty rites of the Zulu tribe. I'm getting off light. I've already decided how to spend the money. Six karate lessons, millions of comic books, and a razor. There's a little fuzz there right now.

(*Does a sexy rendition of the TV commercial.*)

"Take it off, take it all off." It's really not a bad deal. But a Bar Mitzvah, at Leonard's of Great Neck? They won't let me shave but they're all ready to call me a man at the age of thirteen. I don't get it.

(*He exits.*)

VOICE OVER: "THE DEFENSE"

OLDER SON (*Delivered as if to the jury. He carries a martini.*):

I love martinis, and the Beefeaters is so delicious, not to mention these two yummy little olives. Ladies and gentlemen. Two divorce cases, back to back, the first thing in the morning. I've tried to explain to Grace that that kind of scheduling is a drain, but she doesn't understand. She wants a raise. (*real angry*) The bitch. (*He drinks.*) She's got the filing system down so that only she can find anything. When she was sick last week (hah, sick) the office was in a panic. We had to call her every two hours just to find out where the briefs were. Now she wants a raise. (*losing control*) What am I supposed to pay her with? Who wants to pay for a divorce nowadays? You buy a book called *Popular Divorce* for five bucks and you do it yourself.

(*He drinks, calming himself down.*)

Jack, my partner, wants to run for the judgeship again. Two resounding defeats and the schmuck wants to run again. He asked me what I think. What I think? When can I ever tell him or anyone else what I think? (*pause*) Sometimes I am so bored. I put myself against the wall. There is no escape. Cornered, every goddam day.

(*He falls through the door.*)

VOICE OVER: "THE DEFENSE RESTS"

YOUNGER SON (*Younger Son enters smoking a joint. Older Son has a pitcher of martinis, his glass, and a newspaper.*):

Lately, I've been having this feeling that I really need some security—a little responsibility.

OLDER SON: Well, get a job, but don't get married.

YOUNGER SON (*He sits on the table.*):

Don't get married?

OLDER SON: If you saw the divorce case I had today, you'd wonder why anyone got married!

YOUNGER SON: I'm tired of coming home to an empty house—meals alone.

OLDER SON: Marriage has its price and as you know

(*Younger Son chimes in.*)

"Money is Freedom."

(*They chuckle.*)

YOUNGER SON: Two can live as cheaply as one.

OLDER SON (*He talks as he reads his paper.*):

The more people you have to support, the less freedom you have.

YOUNGER SON: Well, I wouldn't mind having someone to share it with.

OLDER SON: Today you can shack up, that's better.

YOUNGER SON (*amazed*): Are you still in love?

OLDER SON (*breaking from the banter*): What?

YOUNGER SON: You heard me—are you still in love?

OLDER SON (*without the slightest consideration*): It's not the same after fourteen years.

YOUNGER SON: Just once, will you please answer my question.

OLDER SON: All right, yes, I am still in love (*pause*) in some ways. Let's face it, you're with someone or you're not. What else is there?

(*Younger Son hands him a joint.*)

No, thanks.

YOUNGER SON: Come on, it might open you up.

OLDER SON: I'll remain closed and stick to my martinis, thank you. Are you ever going to grow up?

YOUNGER SON: No. (*He laughs.*)

OLDER SON: Get off the table, and don't smoke that thing in my house.

YOUNGER SON: Do you lust after younger women?

OLDER SON: No, I don't.

YOUNGER SON: You don't.

OLDER SON: I don't.

YOUNGER SON: You don't?

OLDER SON: I don't? Look, my world is very constant. I don't enjoy living in a state of flux.

YOUNGER SON: Well, don't you ever want to do something different?

OLDER SON (*emphatic*): No!

YOUNGER SON: I don't understand why you don't just enjoy the kids, the job, the responsibility.

OLDER SON: I do.

YOUNGER SON: Well, you hardly act it.

OLDER SON (*angry*): Look, you've got nothing weighing you down. You won't even commit to a bath in the morning, much less a job. You can do whatever you want! Maybe you should start wondering why you're so unhappy.

YOUNGER SON (*defensive*): I'm not unhappy—I'm just chronically subdued.

OLDER SON: You're not subdued—you're drugged.

YOUNGER SON (*on exit*): In California I would be respected for my ability to "lay back."

(*He exits.*)

VOICE OVER: "THE DEFENSE RESTS AGAIN"

Wife calls "Darling" from offstage. Older Son takes a quick drink before she enters.

WIFE: Darling, I'm very upset.

OLDER SON: What is it, sweetheart?

WIFE: Well, I just happened to hear the children arguing—I should say pounding each other—and your daughter just used the word f.u.c.k.

OLDER SON: Not f.u.c.k.?

WIFE: Yes, f.u.c.k.

OLDER SON: Well, what did you say?

WIFE: What did I say? Well, I didn't say anything. I just happened to overhear it—I mean, they weren't in my presence. But we have to reconsider sending them to private school.

OLDER SON: Sweetheart, everyone uses the word "fuck." It's a reality of life. (*joking*) Do you think children in private school only use the word "phooey"?

(*He reads the paper.*)

WIFE: Oh, honestly, your daughter is accosted daily at the bus stop by that Franklin degenerate, and your son, your son may be precocious but he cannot read or write.

(*She grabs his paper.*)

Now he's never going to get into the college of his choice.

OLDER SON: Darling, it's important for them to go to public school.

WIFE: Why?

OLDER SON: They shouldn't be sheltered from society—they should be exposed to it, just as we were. We went to public school and we turned out just fine.

WIFE: Do you seriously think society is the same today as it was when we were in high school?

(*She takes his martini pitcher and glass away, and strikes them in the hutch.*)

Last night on the news, oh this is a lovely story. You'll love this. A teacher discovered a boy and girl going all the way in the school washroom—during school hours.

OLDER SON (*making another joke*): On the floor or on the commode?

WIFE: It's not a joke—they don't do those things in private schools.

OLDER SON: It's too expensive.

WIFE (*Really getting worked up, she grabs his newspaper again and screams.*):

Everything is too expensive! These are your children I'm talking about. What do you expect me to do?

OLDER SON (*explodes*): SWEETHEART—relax. Do as your yogi tells you and take a deep breath. (*poking her*) Do it. Do it.

(*She begins feverishly doing deep yoga breaths.*)

Now isn't that better?

(*She continues breathing but shoots him a look that could kill.*)

They say the fifties are coming back into fashion. Just be patient.

(*She stops the breathing with clenched teeth.*)

VOICE OVER: "IT HAPPENED ONE NIGHT"

The double date. Wife strikes newspaper and pulls menus out from under the table as Girl Friend enters. Older Son gets up to help her into her seat, but she nods him away. There is an awkward silence as they wait for the Younger Son to appear. He finally stumbles onto the scene and slowly makes his way to his seat. After he sits, Wife nudges her husband to get the conversation going.

OLDER SON: How long have you been separated from your husband?

WIFE (*totally embarrassed*): What a question to ask!

GIRL FRIEND (*to Wife*): About two months. (*to Older Son*) Alice tells me you're Jewish and your wife's not. Has that created any adjustment difficulties in the marriage?

WIFE (*stunned*): Where do you practice social work?

OLDER SON: No, she makes a mean gefilte fish.

(*He laughs at his own joke; Younger Son laughs at him laughing.*)

GIRL FRIEND: I work almost exclusively with third-world psychopathic and schizophrenic transsexuals. I think your brother is a manic-depressive with a possible tendency toward schizophrenia. Do you have a dominant Jewish mother?

YOUNGER SON: She's not into leather, if that's what you mean. My sister-in-law tells me you can write prescriptions.

(*Wife gives him an elbow.*)

OLDER SON (*trying to change the subject*): What's the deal with that film . . . I hate subtitles. I mean I have to read all day, who wants to read a movie?

GIRL FRIEND (*to Younger Son*): Are you interested in psycho-pharmacology?

YOUNGER SON: No, I'm interested in better living through chemicals.

OLDER SON: Sonny, I have never understood your fascination with foreign films.

GIRL FRIEND: I must say that I am a sucker for manic-depressive men. They're so easy to cheat on. They even enjoy it.

WIFE (*shocked*): Was your husband a manic-depressive?

GIRL FRIEND: Unfortunately not. Except for an occasional bed wetting, I would classify him as painfully normal.

WIFE: Normal . . . just like mine.

OLDER SON: And that bit with the woman cutting her private parts with a piece of glass. I suppose you find meaning in that?

YOUNGER SON: My brother loves telling me that my life has no meaning. That I haven't found myself yet.

GIRL FRIEND: My experience leads me to believe that if you stopped worrying about what you're going to do with your life, and did something—anything—you would be a lot better off. Now I always tell my patients to get a waiter's job.

(*Older Son moans.*)

It forces them to relate to people on a more regular basis and—

OLDER SON: I wish a waiter would start relating to us on a more regular basis.

(*Signals across the room to a waiter.*)

WIFE: Have you had an opportunity to go to that cute little place that just opened up across the street from Bloomingdale's?

GIRL FRIEND: I don't eat meat.

OLDER SON: I don't chew it.

YOUNGER SON: I think I'm falling in love.

(*Silence.*)

GIRL FRIEND: I hope you're not the type destined to the pattern of falling in love with women who are beyond your reach.

OLDER SON: Are you always this charming and witty?

GIRL FRIEND: One does what one can. Unfortunately, Alice always had better table manners than I.

OLDER SON: Than me.

GIRL FRIEND: Than I.

OLDER SON: Than me.

GIRL FRIEND (*ready to kill*): Than I.

OLDER SON (*returning the sentiment*): Than me, goddamnit.

WIFE: Well, it's a great little restaurant. I had the most lovely quiche lorraine. It only had little tiny bits of ham in it. My yogi, Buba au Rum, is always extolling the virtues of a meatless diet. Do you do yoga?

OLDER SON: No.

WIFE: I know you don't.

GIRL FRIEND: I do Alexander technique.

OLDER SON: I do golf.

WIFE: Oh, I've heard lovely things about that.

YOUNGER SON (*Throwing himself on the table.*):

I know I'm falling in love. The pit of my stomach is hollow. My heart is fluttering. I feel like Clark Gable to your Claudette Colbert.

OLDER SON: She's hardly Claudette Colbert.

WIFE: Times were much simpler then.

GIRL FRIEND: I've learned to live for the moment. Please excuse us.

(*She whispers to the Younger Son.*)

WIFE: But we haven't even ordered supper yet.

GIRL FRIEND: Don't you feel that all too often people conform to social convention at the expense of their honesty?

(*She grabs his hand and pulls him out the nearest exit.*)

OLDER SON: She's a carnivore if ever I saw one.

WIFE: Well, they do make sort of a cute couple.

OLDER SON (*desperately yelling across the room*): I'll have a double martini up, two olives! Now!

WIFE: Do you remember our first date?

OLDER SON: Oh yes. It was a slushy day in the middle of February. You were wearing open-toed sandals.

WIFE (*embarrassed*): Oh golly, we were so happy. And you were wearing English Leather. And they were playing Frank Sinatra. (*Heavy sigh.*)

(*Suddenly Frank Sinatra singing "Embraceable You" or the like comes up in the background. The Wife and Older Son stop dead, then suddenly look around in the space bewildered. Older Son takes charge. He flings his menu on the table, straightens his tie, and gets up from his seat going to the Wife and taking her by the hand, bringing her downstage. He takes her in his arms. She swoons. They begin to dance. It is a rather tentative effort—the box step. He gets adventurous. He tries for a dip. He slips, the Wife yells and the two go tumbling about as the lights black out.*)

VOICE OVER: "MINCING WORDS"

MOTHER (*Reading from the cookbook.*):

"Many Jewish customs center about the table where the family meet. This is especially true of holidays. The Jewish table may be said to be the center of the home; its altar of friendship, and, if properly provisioned, the family's source of strength and health. Jewish women have ever forged the golden links in the eternal chain. Be you a link transmitting and joining to future generations or a golden charm adding to the beauty of our heritage, it is through the works of your hands in your home that we as a people will continue to survive."

(*She closes the cover and reads.*)

"*Sisterhood Cookbook*, Temple Beth El, Swampscott, Massachusetts."

VOICE OVER: "WHEN YOU KISS"

Granddaughter sitting at table, reading aloud from magazine.

GRANDDAUGHTER: "Studies show that pressures on adolescent women are often sexual as well as social. Today, average teen boys have high expectations when dating girls of the same age, or even younger. Peer group pressure has resulted in activities that go beyond the expected excursions into necking and petting, often advancing to sophisticated foreplay and sometimes beyond to even more kinky behavior." Kinky behavior? GROSS!

(*Makes a face and calls offstage.*)

Mom? Mommy!

(*Wife enters with bowl of potatoes, which she peels throughout the scene.*)

WIFE: Uh huh.

GRANDDAUGHTER: Tell me how you and Daddy met.

WIFE (*She sits next to daughter.*):

Well, we were at one of those frat mixers, and he was on one side of the room and I was on the other side.

GRANDDAUGHTER: Was it love at first sight?

WIFE: Oh, of course not. I don't believe in that.

GRANDDAUGHTER: Well, what happened?

WIFE: Let's see. I remember being introduced to him, and thinking he was very attractive and very charming.

GRANDDAUGHTER: Did you kiss?

WIFE: No honey, we just met. I was with another fellow.

GRANDDAUGHTER: How long was it before you got married?

WIFE: Oh, let's see. I was a sophomore and he was a junior. About a year and a half.

GRANDDAUGHTER: Did you love him when you got married?

WIFE: What do you think?

GRANDDAUGHTER: How long was it before you had me?

WIFE (*flustered*): We were blessed with you in the first year.

GRANDDAUGHTER: Well, when you kissed him, what was it like?

WIFE: Oh, it was very special.

GRANDDAUGHTER: Did he stick his tongue in your mouth?

WIFE (*aghast*): . . . What!

GRANDDAUGHTER: Well, when did you first let him touch you?

WIFE: . . . I don't remember.

GRANDDAUGHTER: Mom.

WIFE (*Growing more nervous as she peels the potatoes.*):
Yes I do, we held hands all the way home after the first date.

GRANDDAUGHTER (*annoyed*): I know that. (*insistent*) I mean when did he . . . you know what I mean.

WIFE: No, honey, I don't know what you mean.

GRANDDAUGHTER: Well, when did he . . . touch you somewhere private.

WIFE (*In a state of shock, she grabs the magazine and scolds.*): I don't want you reading these magazines anymore!

GRANDDAUGHTER (*tearful*): Well if you would talk to me I wouldn't have to read them.

WIFE: Oh, that pot roast.

(*She begins to exit.*)

GRANDDAUGHTER: Mommy!

WIFE: I have a little book I want you to read.

(*She makes a quick exit.*)

GRANDDAUGHTER: Thanks!

VOICE OVER: "THE GRANDDAUGHTER BREAKS OUT"

GRANDDAUGHTER (*In a rage first to her mother offstage, then to the audience.*):

Stephen Franklin keeps picking on me at the bus stop. I don't want to ride the bus anymore. Please don't make me ride the bus. In the last two weeks, I've had to fake being sick four times, just so I wouldn't have to ride the bus with him. I hate boys. They think they can do whatever they want just because they're boys. I never see my father. He doesn't even talk to me until he drinks that stink-pot pitcher full of smell. All the other girls in my class, well, they've had their period for months and months. All the other girls are starting to develop. Thank goodness for Jenny. At least we can talk. At least we can be close friends. I'm just so damned tired of school! I can't wait for the summer. Then I can baby-sit and make some money. Daddy says "money is freedom." There is this great big pimple pressing on my forehead. I hope it doesn't come out until the weekend. Otherwise that asshole Stephen Franklin will make fun of me all the way to school. Well, if I have to suffer the pain of pimples, the least I could do is get my period. I don't want to be different!

VOICE OVER: "LET'S MAKE A DEAL"

Grandson enters with a portable television. They have this discussion as they watch TV at the table.

GRANDSON: I just don't get it.

GRANDDAUGHTER: We have got to give him a birthday gift, that's all there is to it.

GRANDSON: Yeah, but why should we take the allowance money he gives us to buy him a gift he isn't even going to like?

GRANDDAUGHTER: Look, I really think we should give him a gold necklace.

GRANDSON: Where are you going to get a gold necklace that we can afford?

GRANDDAUGHTER: They're selling them on the street. They say they're genuinely gold. I'll buy one and put it in one of Mom's Bloomingdale's boxes and he'll think we got it there. It's only seven dollars.

GRANDSON: And you think he's going to wear a gold necklace?

GRANDDAUGHTER: Lots of older men are wearing them. They're sexy.

GRANDSON: Well, he's not sexy and he's not going to wear a necklace.

GRANDDAUGHTER (*getting pissed*): All right. So he'll wear it for a few days so we won't feel bad and then he'll stick it in his drawer and that will be that.

GRANDSON: What a waste.

GRANDDAUGHTER: It's not a waste. I've been dying for a gold necklace. And when he puts it in his drawer and forgets about it, I'll take it out and I'll wear it.

GRANDSON (*angry*): You're going to wear a man's necklace?

(*He stands up.*)

GRANDDAUGHTER (*She stands up.*):
It's unisexual.

GRANDSON (*ready for combat*): I'm not paying half if you're going to wear it.

GRANDDAUGHTER: You are such a runt. And cheap too.

(*She picks him up in a bear hug. When she puts him down he mocks a karate chop in her direction, then sits down at the table —one eye on her, one eye on the television.*)

GRANDDAUGHTER (*trying a loving tact*): Buddy . . . buddy . . . you pay half now and when the time comes that I get to wear the necklace, I'll pay you back half, okay?

GRANDSON (*Pushes her away.*):
You're shrewd.

GRANDDAUGHTER: I'm just being practical.

(*She grabs the TV as she gives him a smack. He attempts a karate yelp.*)

GRANDDAUGHTER (*returning the yelp*): You little pygmy!

GRANDSON: Micro-boobs!

(*He flies under the table.*)

VOICE OVER: "FUTURE TENSE"

Older Son enters with a martini and the evening paper and sits down at the table. As he puts the drink down, the Grandson bumps the table from underneath, spilling the drink.

OLDER SON: Why do you insist on hiding under the table?

GRANDSON (*as he comes out*): I'm not hiding, I'm playing.

OLDER SON: Why don't you play in the playroom I spent a small fortune on remodeling for that express purpose? You're too old to be behaving in such an abnormal manner.

GRANDSON (*He comes over and hangs on his father's shoulder.*): What's so abnormal about hiding and playing?

OLDER SON: Hiding under the dining room table is not what a boy of your age should be doing.

GRANDSON: Well, what did you do when you were my age?

OLDER SON: I was a Boy Scout. Why don't you become a Boy Scout?

GRANDSON: I'd look lousy in a uniform!

OLDER SON: Don't be rude. The Boy Scouts would make a man out of you.

GRANDSON: I thought having a Bar Mitzvah was going to make a man out of me.

OLDER SON (*Back to his paper.*): Don't you have some home-work to do?

GRANDSON: What about your brother? What did he do as a kid?

OLDER SON (*hesitates*): He hid under the table, but he was a very peculiar child.

GRANDSON: How come you're so different—being brothers and all?

OLDER SON: I think your grandmother dropped him on his head when he was a baby.

(*They both laugh.*)

He just hasn't found himself yet.

GRANDSON: What's to find?

OLDER SON: He's just in a state of flux.

GRANDSON: What's a state of flux?

OLDER SON: An expression of speech.

GRANDSON: What's an expression of speech?

(*He sticks his finger in the martini.*)

OLDER SON (*smacking his arm*): Are you trying to drive me crazy?

GRANDSON (*He sits down.*):

Dad, can I tell you something very important?

OLDER SON: Yeah, sure.

(*Drinks the martini.*)

GRANDSON: You see, there's this really sexy blonde from down South who's the Assistant Principal's secretary,

(*Older Son sees a big tale coming and goes back to reading the paper.*)

and I was walking past her office and our eyes met for an instant, and I thought, what the hell, I'll give it a whirl. So I went in and we made lots of small talk, and she said, "Would you all like to come over to my house after school?" And I said, "Sure, I get out of science at the end of seventh period, I'll come over then." So I went over to her apartment after school and she came to the door in this sexy black nightgown, like in *Playboy* magazine.

(*Older Son mumbles* "Uh huh.")

And I walked inside and she gave me this really juicy kiss, you know the kind you have to wipe your mouth after. Then she said, "Buddy, can I get you all a drink?" and I said, "Sure." So when she went into the other room to get me a drink, I happened to see on her coffee table this big white book, and I started looking in it and it turned out to be a wedding album, and I realized, I was in some married woman's house, and she was wearing a skimpy black negligee and her husband might walk in any minute and catch us in the middle of doing something "unkosher." So I got out of there as fast as I could because if he got jealous he might shoot me or stab me and I wouldn't want to embarrass the family with a big scandal, you know what I mean?

OLDER SON: That's very thoughtful of you, Buddy. You're a funny kid, you know that?

(*Drinks the martini.*)

GRANDSON: I think I have a special gift for comedy—at least that's what my teacher told me.

OLDER SON: Oh, really?

GRANDSON: Yeah, I think I want to write for television when I grow up.

OLDER SON: Television? (*with some disdain*) That's an exciting and lucrative profession.

GRANDSON: Make some commercials. I have some very exciting ideas for selling cereal.

OLDER SON: I love law. It's so reasonable. The whole notion of precedence and legal history. You walk into a court of law and you know what to expect. You walk into your house at the end of the day and who the hell knows what you're up against?

(*Granddaughter enters and sets the table. Wife can hand her things through the dutch door.*)

The kid says he wants to go into television. He's likely to change his mind. Take antitrust, for example, now that's as exciting a concern as selling cereal. All those big guys ganging up on all of us little guys. Who could be against the breaking of a trust? No, his mind will change a dozen times. You'll see.

VOICE OVER: "THE EVENING MEAL"

As the lights come up the Grandson starts playing a calypso beat on the plates with his silverware. Older Son is glued to his newspaper but mutters, "Buddy, Buddy" trying to get him to stop. Finally he yells "Stop it" at the same time the Granddaughter grabs the silverware away from him.

WIFE (*from offstage*): What's going on in there?

OLDER SON: Nothing, sweetheart.

(*Silently, the Grandson and Granddaughter begin to pinch each other under the table. The Granddaughter lands a good one. The Grandson yelps "Ouch" and the Older Son yells "Stop it" again. He goes back to his paper and, smiling, the kids lock hands under the table. Silently they fight, each bending the other's fingers. Their heads lock against each other. They begin to moan. Older Son: "I'm warning you. Stop it." He finally reels around and smacks the Granddaughter hard on the head with the newspaper, breaking up the fight. Wife makes a speedy entrance oblivious to the conflict.*)

WIFE (*entering*): Did you tell your father your surprise?

GRANDDAUGHTER (*with venom*): No!

OLDER SON: Mommy tells me that you were chosen to be on the cheerleading squad.

GRANDDAUGHTER (*snotty*): Uh huh.

OLDER SON (*losing patience*): That's very nice.

WIFE (*to grandson*): What do you think about that?

GRANDSON (*smiling*): That's great.

(*He reaches in front of Granddaughter for casserole.*)

Pass the potatoes.

WIFE: Don't you say please?

GRANDSON: Please.

WIFE: Eat your vegetables first.

OLDER SON: Darling, do I smell something burning?

WIFE: My God! The vegetables.

(*Exits to kitchen.*)

OLDER SON: Oh, great.

(*Older Son goes to the hutch for a martini refill. Grandson turns to Granddaughter and silently mouths "Fuck you." She mouths something back and suddenly the Grandson grabs the Granddaughter by the neck and inflicts a powerful head lock. The Granddaughter turns beet red and begins to moan as if she is choking. Older Son has his fresh martini, stops with the hutch door in hand; seething, he slams it as hard as he can. The kids break immediately. Wife cheerfully enters with the charred vegetables. She looks at Older Son to wonder why he slammed the door. He points to the kids, who look angelic and smile innocently at the mother. Wife signals Older Son to talk to Granddaughter.*)

OLDER SON: How many girls were chosen for the squad?

GRANDDAUGHTER: Forty. But I'm the only one who can do a split.

GRANDSON: Now can I have the vegetables?

OLDER SON: Can't you say please?

GRANDSON: Please.

(*The following lines come in a quick succession, building to the Granddaughter's exit.*)

WIFE: Tell your father what Miss Perceverse said.

GRANDDAUGHTER: Miss Perceverse said if I can keep my grades up I might make varsity next year.

OLDER SON: That will be great for your college applications.

GRANDSON: Where are you going tomorrow night?

WIFE: To the movies with your uncle.

OLDER SON (*pained*): Again?

GRANDDAUGHTER: Does he have a date?

WIFE: Yes. Alice's sister.

GRANDSON: I thought she just got married.

GRANDDAUGHTER: Can Jenny come over tomorrow night?

OLDER SON: Is she divorced yet?

WIFE: Yes, but please stay out of my makeup.

GRANDSON: Can Nathaniel come over? I don't want to be alone with them.

GRANDDAUGHTER: No, Daddy, they'll drive us crazy all night.

OLDER SON: We'll see. Does her husband have a lawyer?

WIFE (*getting angry*): I don't know.

GRANDSON: They just want to smoke cigarettes.

WIFE: What!?

GRANDDAUGHTER (*Lunges toward him with intent to kill.*):
You brat!
(*Smacks him.*)
We don't smoke. (*crying*) No one understands me and no one even tries.
(*She slams her fist on the table and then runs out of the room screaming.*)

OLDER SON (*Unfazed and with a martini poised for action.*):
Why is that child so high strung?

WIFE: It's just a phase.

GRANDSON (*insistent*): Can I have some potatoes?

WIFE and OLDER SON (*frazzled*): Can't you say please?

GRANDSON (*yells*): PLEASE!

OLDER SON (*angry*): What is it with you and whipped potatoes?

GRANDSON (*angelic*): It reminds me of shaving cream.

WIFE and OLDER SON: Shaving cream?
(*Loud crash and scream from the Granddaughter is heard offstage. Grandson disappears under table.*)

OLDER SON (*to Wife*): Your children are very strange.

WIFE: Oh, I'm glad to see you've finally noticed.

(*Moving to her daughter offstage.*)

Cookie, have you finished throwing your fit in there? Can't we have one meal in peace?

OLDER SON: Excuse me, dear.

(*He exits.*)

WIFE (*She can't believe he's leaving the table, then notices her son is gone, too.*):

Buddy? Buddy?

VOICE OVER: "SUNNYSIDE UP"

Commercial music comes up in the background. Wife picks the napkins off the table and begins doing her deep yoga breathing. The breathing exercise turns her grimace to a smile. She gives this speech as she clears the table.

WIFE: I've always been happy. Always. Oh, sure, there was a time when even I gave into depression. But really, there's no question about it. I'm just a happy person by nature. Now that can threaten some people.

(*She looks around the space to indicate the "some people" as her family.*)

Sometimes when I have a smile on my face they ask me "What's the matter?" Like if I'm just in a merry mood, there has to be a reason. I'm just simple-minded! Now there's a lot to be said for simplicity. I don't claim to feel less than anyone else. Sure, I have my bad days, but I let go. I get angry, and that's that. I don't make things complex when they can be simple and easy. I feel pain, but I don't dwell on it. I think of things that make me happy. Unlike some people I know, I count my blessings and not my problems. Take my mother-in-law, for instance. All that woman seems to talk about is this one's stomach cancer, and that one's cataract operation and who's divorcing who.

(*She takes the plastic glasses, the last items to be cleared, and throws them through the open dutch door in a fit. She then grabs a coffee cup and without losing a beat or her smile continues her speech.*)

And my husband is forever glued to his newspaper—sometimes I think that man would rather read about political unrest and crime than be with his own family. And the kids. Children, our one hope for the future—last night I joined them in the TV room. They were watching this gruesome program about starving people, in Indo-Asia—or somewhere! Well, I just shut that television off and said, "For crying out loud, can't you kids watch something a little cheerier? Whatever happened to 'Ozzie and Harriet?'" Well, those kids looked at me like I was nuts. Listen, I just try to smile and bring a little happiness into this family. I mean, we're all going to end up with six feet of ground on top of us, let's have a few laughs. But you know, some people see the cup of life as half empty. I see it as half full. And if those half empties won't let us half fulls be happy. (*angry*) Fuck 'em.

(*Blackout.*)

VOICE OVER: "COMING TO TERMS"

Younger Son and Girl Friend enter from opposite sides. His shirt is off. She is wearing it as her top. They smoke a joint.

YOUNGER SON (*unusually chipper*): Boy, that was really great.

GIRL FRIEND (*embarrassed*): Yes. It was beautiful.

YOUNGER SON: You're very soft. (*She doesn't react.*)

It always makes me feel so much better. You know, one of life's great organic tranquilizers.

GIRL FRIEND (*to the audience*): The last thing I want is to get involved with this guy. My freedom is so important to me now. God, how could I have been so naive to get married to that creep? I am so embarrassed when I think that I said I would love him forever. What was I doing? Please don't try to make me love you. The sex is good, that's all I ask for now. Can't you be satisfied with that? Please don't press me for more. I just came out of a painful relationship. (*pause*) So what if we were only married for forty-three days. We lived together for six months before that. My mother thought he was wonderful. (*pause*) No, of course I don't blame it on my mother. I just wanted to get out, I guess, and he was the closest ticket. Oh, he meant well. I don't believe he loved me. He says he did. He cried when I said I was leaving. One whole year without getting my period. That says something. I'm away from him for a week and boom, it comes right back. Regular. Relief.

YOUNGER SON: It always makes me feel so much better. You know, one of life's great organic tranquilizers.

GIRL FRIEND (*annoyed*): Do you always feel compelled to talk about it?

YOUNGER SON (*hurt*): No, not always.

GIRL FRIEND: I have this patient who can only get it off if there's the sound of dripping water coming from the bathroom.

YOUNGER SON: Why?

GIRL FRIEND: It has to do with his mother.

YOUNGER SON (*to the audience*): God, I've tried to figure it out a million times. I decided it all has to do with the movies and television. This cliché romantic notion. Like in *It Happened One Night*. The Romeo and Juliet syndrome. Boy meets Girl. Boy and Girl have a humorous and exciting adventure. Boy asks Girl to marry. A big wedding in a tent with lots of gifts and checks. Boy and Girl buy a split-level tract. Boy and Girl have two kids, one boy, one girl. Peter and Wendy. Boy and Girl get older, get fatter, get bored, get divorced, have an ugly custody battle. Wendy disappears. Jaded. They all say I'm jaded.

GIRL FRIEND: I have this patient who can only get it off if there's the sound of dripping water coming from the bathroom.

YOUNGER SON: Why?

GIRL FRIEND: It has to do with his mother.

YOUNGER SON: You really believe that crap?

GIRL FRIEND: Absolutely.

YOUNGER SON: I really think love and hate are very similar emotions.

GIRL FRIEND: I'm an eclectic by nature. A little Jung. A touch of Freud. Rollo May. Karen Horney. And of course, we musn't forget Dr. David Rubin.

YOUNGER SON: Do you think anyone would ever make a movie about people like us?

GIRL FRIEND: A play maybe, but never a movie. (*to the audience*) He's so cute. And not as crazy as he thinks, and he is kind. But it's important for me to have time to myself . . . to have a sense of my own freedom. I know it sounds cliché, but I'll only hurt him.

(*She exits.*)

YOUNGER SON (*to the audience*): Boy is in love with Girl, but she's not interested. She wants to be free. I should type into my computer key punch "Casual Affair." I know that if she were available I wouldn't care so much. I know if she wanted to move in tomorrow I would freak out. I know these things. If only it happened one night. If only I was a poor immigrant from Minsk and one had no choice. If only I had a job that mattered more than anything in the world. Money is not freedom. Frontal lobotomies are freedom.

(*He exits.*)

VOICE OVER: "THE DILEMMA"

GRANDAUGHTER (*She dashes in wearing Dr. Denton's.*):

I know you're going to find this hard to believe, but Stephen Franklin, of all people, has invited me to the freshman prom. I just can't believe it. He's been so mean to me for so long. He told me it was his way of expressing affection. Can you imagine? He's continually embarrassed me, practically tortured me in front of my peers, and now he thinks I am going to be his escort to the social event of the season. Jenny says I should go with him. Mommy will just throw a fit when I tell her. Jenny says it's because I made the cheering squad. Stephen was impressed when he heard I could do a split and was chosen for the cheering squad. I really don't know what to say. He is kind of cute, but a woman must have her pride. All the other girls are going to the dance. I'll just die if no one invites me. As Grandma says, *Nisht Gefidelt!*

(*Exits.*)

VOICE OVER: "SONS AND LOVERS"

Mother and Younger Son enter. Younger Son is carrying two large shopping bags which he takes directly to the kitchen.

MOTHER: Oh, Sonny, I don't know what I would do without you.

YOUNGER SON: You'd pay somebody to carry your groceries home.

MOTHER: Oi, you're such a good boy. Would you like a delicious piece of cake?

YOUNGER SON: Sure.

MOTHER: Then go wash up!

YOUNGER SON (*He sits.*):
I am washed.

(*She gives him a look and brings the cake to the table.*)

MOTHER: I had a dream last night, Sonny. Your father came to me. He told me he was very upset that you were still living off his money and not working and earning a living of your own.

YOUNGER SON: Well, tonight, when you go to sleep, tell him that the money is almost gone.

MOTHER (*aghast*): No!

YOUNGER SON: Yes!

(*He eats the cake.*)

MOTHER: So what happens if you meet a nice girl, and you want a little money to start raising a family and making a home?

YOUNGER SON: I'm sorry, Ma.

MOTHER: All right. Tell me what you want to do? You want to be a lawyer like your brother?

(*He laughs.*)

A doctor?

(*She laughs back.*)

No, it's too late for that. How about a program computerer?

YOUNGER SON: How about a waiter?

MOTHER: You went to college so that you could be a waiter?

YOUNGER SON (*a little nasty*): I went to college so I wouldn't have to have this conversation when I got out of high school.

MOTHER (*She continues to ignore his testiness.*):
So at least try graduate school. You might like it.

YOUNGER SON: What about Bellevue Psychiatric?

MOTHER: I only want to see you happy. You mope so much.

YOUNGER SON: I hear they have open admissions at Odyssey House.

MOTHER: What kind of House?

YOUNGER SON: Drugs, Ma, for drug addicts.

MOTHER (*she laughs*): You're such a handsome, such a virile boy. If only you were as industrious as you were handsome . . .

YOUNGER SON: I've got it! The Masters and Johnson Clinic!

MOTHER: What kind of clinic?

YOUNGER SON: Masters and Johnson . . . Sex, Mom. It's a sex clinic.

MOTHER (*aghast*): Oh, honey, you've got . . . sexual hang-ups?

YOUNGER SON: No, Mom, I was just kidding.

MOTHER: But you do like girls?

YOUNGER SON: Girls?

MOTHER: Girls.

YOUNGER SON: Girls.

MOTHER: Girls.

YOUNGER SON: Well, I don't know about girls . . .

MOTHER: You don't know about girls?

YOUNGER SON: Don't you think I'm a little old for girls?

MOTHER: But you like Alice's sister?

YOUNGER SON: I mean a person of the female sex over the age of 18 likes to be called a woman—

MOTHER: You invite Alice's sister over for dinner and I'm gonna fix a nice flanken . . .

YOUNGER SON: Maybe I do like little baby girls . . .

MOTHER: Good! You bring that girl over and I'll fix everything up just fine.

YOUNGER SON: Look, why don't *you* go back to graduate school and I'll make the flanken.

(*Younger Son exits in a fit of frustration.*)

VOICE OVER: "THE MOTHER'S LAMENT"

MOTHER (*to the audience as she clears the table*): He's a good kid. He still has a bit of the child in him, if you know what I mean. He doesn't really need me to watch over him, but my mind would be at rest if he had a profession and a wife to take care of him. Security. A steady source of income. "Money is Freedom." I don't understand why he didn't learn about that in college. Education today prepares you for nothing. This is no easy life. A person needs some help. You have to be tough to get ahead. A person could get tossed by the wayside . . . lost in the crowd. Listen, people don't care about each other anymore. It's still a dog world. It always will be. Look, he's a nice guy, don't misunderstand me, but unfortunately, nice guys always finish last. Am I right?

(*She exits.*)

VOICE OVER: "THE BAR MITZVAH"

Grandson appears from behind closed doors. There is cantoral music in the background. He is wearing a spangled prayer shawl and skull cap over a white tux or the like. He begins his speech in traditional Bar Mitzvah fashion.

GRANDSON: On this, my Bar Mitzvah day, I come before you in gratitude, humility, and resolution as I look ahead to my service as an adult member of the Jewish community. I accept the responsibility that this religious ritual offers and I look forward to meeting the challenge that lies ahead for our religion, in this troubled society. I wish to take this opportunity to thank my loving parents without whose support and guidance I would be unable to stand before you now. I also wish to thank my dear uncle for the Schick Super Deluxe Double Edge Razor; my sweet sister, for her gift of a gold lamé unisex disco shirt (that's a little too large); and of course, my beloved grandmother, for the solid gold monogram cuff links and the large check which has been deposited in a joint account with my father and will become solely mine on the occasion of my twenty-first birthday.

(Assumes a more aggressive stance somewhere between a politician and a rock star.)

But let me make one last thing perfectly clear. I'll fight compromise and corruption. I'll stand for the Semitic-American way of life. I'll even give to the U.J.A. Although I may continue to act as a childlike person, on this my Bar Mitzvah day, I pledge to be sincerely as unchildish as possible from now on.

(Hallelujah chorus disco music bumps up. Older Son joins Grandson and gives him a cereal bowl, then poses for a flash photograph. Granddaughter can take pictures downstage. Mother dashes in carrying a box of Fruit Loops which she pours into the bowl after giving the little boy a huge kiss. They pose for a

photograph. Wife enters carrying a milk bowl which she pours on top of the cereal after posing for a photograph. Grandson eats cereal as they pose for a family photo. Suddenly, Girl Friend enters in a blond wig and black negligee and gives Grandson a hot kiss. Then she covers his face with shaving cream, purring "take it off, take it all off." She dashes off and the Grandson follows in close pursuit. The rest of the family stand bewildered as lights black out.)

VOICE OVER: "CUT FROM THE SAME CLOTH"

GRANDDAUGHTER (*Younger Son sits at the table and watches Granddaughter cheer.*):

Watch this, Uncle Sonny—Go, go, where, where, we want a touchdown over there, yea, team!

(*She joins him at table and shows him a book.*)

That's me in my yearbook.

(*Younger Son reads aloud from Granddaughter's school yearbook.*)

YOUNGER SON: Nickname: "Cookie." Favorite quote: "Money is Freedom." Oh, Cookie, how could you?

GRANDDAUGHTER (*defensively*): Well, I couldn't think of anything else!

YOUNGER SON (*continues reading*): "Energetic cheerleader and faithful friend of Miss Perceverse's Pep Club. Baby sitting and the beach in summer. According to our Cookie: "Everybody looks better with a tan. . . . Future looks hazy after High School, but college and marriage appear somewhere on the horizon." Aren't you a little young to be thinking about marriage?

GRANDDAUGHTER: I don't know. Aren't *you* ever going to get married?

YOUNGER SON: You sound like your Grandmother.

GRANDDAUGHTER: Cut my tongue out.

YOUNGER SON: She's a good old lady.

GRANDDAUGHTER: Sometimes she nags.

YOUNGER SON: Sometimes you whine.

GRANDDAUGHTER: Why does she always make you eat?

YOUNGER SON: It's her form of self-expression.

GRANDDAUGHTER: You always have to be on your guard when she kisses you. Last week she kissed me so hard she left a hickey.

(*They both laugh.*)

YOUNGER SON: Are you sure some boy didn't leave it?

GRANDDAUGHTER: Ugh! No! (*pause*) Uncle Sonny, were you mean to girls when you were young?

YOUNGER SON: Cookie, I was mean to everyone.

GRANDDAUGHTER: Why?

YOUNGER SON: I don't know. When you get old enough to think about it, you get embarrassed and stop. You're mean to Grandma.

GRANDDAUGHTER: I am not.

YOUNGER SON: Yeah, you are. You're just too young to know it.

GRANDDAUGHTER: Well, I'm going through adolescence!

YOUNGER SON: What are you going to do after adolescence?

GRANDDAUGHTER: I don't know. All I'm looking forward to is being alone with my very own phone.

YOUNGER SON: No, come on.

GRANDDAUGHTER: I don't know! Maybe a dermatologist.

YOUNGER SON: A dermatologist? (*He laughs.*)

GRANDDAUGHTER (*hurt*): Daddy says you haven't found yourself yet.

YOUNGER SON: I am enjoying the search, and you can tell your father that.

GRANDDAUGHTER: I don't know what the big deal is. I mean, you're not a mass murderer or a rapist, right?

YOUNGER SON: Wrong. (*He laughs.*)

GRANDDAUGHTER: You are a little weird sometimes, but I think you're cute and real funny.

YOUNGER SON: You're very pretty, you know that? (*She shrugs.*) Do you have any boyfriends?

GRANDDAUGHTER: No, not really.

YOUNGER SON: Would you like to have one?

GRANDDAUGHTER: I don't know. I guess so.

YOUNGER SON (*leans over and says in mocking fashion*): Hey, sweetheart, how would you like to catch a couple of beers and a drive-in and—

GRANDDAUGHTER (*shocked*): That's disgusting!
(*She grabs her book and starts to exit.*)

YOUNGER SON: I was just kidding.

GRANDDAUGHTER: You're a member of the family. UGH!

(*She exits.*)

YOUNGER SON (*stunned and to the audience*): No one understands me. No one even tries.

(*He exits.*)

VOICE OVER: "ANTITRUST"

Older Son enters wearing boxer shorts, a worn robe, black socks, and old slippers. He is carrying a magazine, chuckling as he reads. He sits at the table. Wife appears from a closed door in a baggy nightgown, cold cream over her face and carrying Kleenex.

WIFE: Darling, aren't you coming to bed?

OLDER SON: I was just reading this magazine of yours.

WIFE (*She goes over to him.*):

That's not my magazine. (*indignant*) I confiscated that from your daughter.

OLDER SON (*he reads*): "Is your married sex life what it should be? Studies show, in order to have a successful marriage that will stand the test of time, it is absolutely essential for couples to discuss their most intimate sexual fantasies."

WIFE: Oh, sweetheart, stop.

OLDER SON (*he continues*): "Conclusive tests show that the inability of couples to open themselves up to such discussions can cost them their blissful bond."

WIFE: You and everybody else believe absolutely everything you read!

OLDER SON: I'm a lawyer.

WIFE: What does that have to do with anything?

OLDER SON: I think we should take this thing seriously. Now tell Daddy your most intimate sexual fantasies.

WIFE: Don't be silly. I don't have any fantasies.

OLDER SON: Sweetness, this article says that it's normal for everyone to have sexual fantasies.

WIFE: Normal! Oh, for crying out loud.

OLDER SON: Well . . .

WIFE: Are you serious?

OLDER SON: Uh huh.

WIFE (*She thinks for a moment, then begins to giggle. Older Son giggles too.*):

Well . . . I never told you this . . . but Alice and Ernie went to this great honeymoon hotel . . . (*Older Son starts to sour*) and they had a waterbed . . . (*Older Son interjects a* "Sweetheart") and a mirror (*Older Son:* "Sweetheart") and they even had a closed circuit TV . . .

OLDER SON: Sweetheart!

WIFE (*annoyed*): What!

OLDER SON: That is not a sexual fantasy. That's just an expensive vacation.

WIFE (*curt*): Okay, Daddy, you tell me what's a sexual fantasy.

OLDER SON: You know, like if I wanted to dress up in women's clothes, for example, or—

WIFE (*stunned*): What? Is that why you like to buy me clothes?

OLDER SON (*laughing off the implication*): That was just a hypothetical supposition.

WIFE: That is not normal. Are you going to sit there and tell me you believe that trash, and that dressing like a woman is normal?

OLDER SON: They're fantasies. Like "make believe." Remember "make believe"?

WIFE (*bitter*): Yes, I remember make believe. Okay, I'll tell you my sexual fantasy—I "make believe" that you give up martinis as your hobby.

OLDER SON (*taken aback*): What?

WIFE: You heard me.

(*She moves away from him.*)

You know you're not exactly the sexual tiger I met at the old frat mixer.

OLDER SON: Well, honey, I mean . . . look at you. That crap on your face every night—and that nightie.

WIFE (*defensive*): You said you like this nightie. What do you want, a black negligee? Look at you!

OLDER SON: All I meant was occasionally I would like to be stirred up by the wonders I know are lurking beneath that flannel sack.

WIFE (*shocked*): You would?

OLDER SON: Yeah. You want a sexual tiger, huh?

WIFE: Oh, I was just kidding . . . (*giggles*)

OLDER SON: No, you said you wanted a sexual tiger. You got it now . . . Grrr . . .

(*Older Son begins making tiger noises. Suddenly he drops to the floor and begins charging the Wife growling on all fours. She protests: "Don't be ridiculous . . . get up." He grabs the nightie with his teeth and pulls her upstage toward the back of the table. She resists at first, then sort of gets into it when he suddenly lets go of her nightie and jumps to his feet.*)

OLDER SON: Wait . . .

WIFE: What?

OLDER SON: I've got a better idea.

WIFE: What?

OLDER SON: We go under the table.

WIFE: What?!

OLDER SON: This magazine says it's good to do those kinds of things—discovery . . . exploration . . .

WIFE: You're joking?

(*He shakes head no.*)

Under the table?

(*He nods yes.*)

OLDER SON: Yeah. Right under.

WIFE: Only if you give up drinking martinis.

OLDER SON: Forever?

WIFE (*she weighs the alternatives*): For now.

OLDER SON: Sure, for now.

(*They start under table.*)

Ah, ah—hair curlers!

(*Wife retreats to open door where she throws Kleenex and curlers offstage. She turns back slowly and responds with a feline growl of her own. He gets excited. Slowly they come together growling and pawing at each other as they slip down behind the table. They no sooner get down when the Grandson in his pajamas pops up between them embarrassed and takes off. Wife freaks out and runs to the open door. Older Son first tries to catch Grandson who has made it out of the room. He turns to Wife only to see her fleeing. He shakes his head grabbing magazine and glasses and splits on blackout.*)

VOICE OVER: "SWEET AND SOUR"

Mother and Girl Friend enter from offstage.

MOTHER: So what do you think?

GIRL FRIEND (*polite*): It's a very nice kitchen.

MOTHER: It's a little old-fashioned, but I like it that way.

GIRL FRIEND: You could certainly sell that ice box as an antique.

MOTHER: Well, sweetheart, God forbid the electricity should go out. Sit down, darling.

GIRL FRIEND: No, thanks. I've really got to run.

MOTHER: You don't like to cook, do you?

GIRL FRIEND: No I don't! I usually eat raw vegetables. You know cooking food depletes it of their minerals and vitamins.

MOTHER: Oh, I see. Now what exactly is it that you said you do for a living?

GIRL FRIEND: I'm a psychiatric social worker.

MOTHER: That's very impressive: so what does it mean?

GIRL FRIEND: Well, I counsel people—help them with their problems.

MOTHER: How lovely. I discuss people's problems all day, and I'm lucky if I get a thank you. (*change of tone*) They pay you well for this work?

GIRL FRIEND: Enough to get along.

MOTHER: Well, Money is—

GIRL FRIEND: FREEDOM. (*She smiles.*) I think it's time for a new family homily.

MOTHER (*Pulls her to a chair.*):
Sit down, sweetheart. How old are you, darling?

GIRL FRIEND (*annoyed*): Twenty-eight.

MOTHER (*They both sit.*):
You're a little older than my son!

GIRL FRIEND: I'm not that much older!

MOTHER: Ah, when I was your age, I had one child, two miscarriages and a partial cleaning out. You don't want to wait too long before having a family. You know what I mean?

GIRL FRIEND: I know exactly what you mean. But I'm in no rush. I can't imagine myself as a wife again, let alone a mother. Times have changed.

MOTHER: Honey, I've been through plenty of change. In my day, people knew what they wanted out of life. Today, young people spend all their time thinking, God forbid anybody should *do* something!

GIRL FRIEND: Now you have to keep an historical perspective when you make those sweeping remarks.

MOTHER: I know I'm only a reminder of the past. Maybe I should be a memory already. (*She looks for a response but doesn't get one.*) You're a sweet girl. A little cool, perhaps, but

I'd be proud to have you in my family. You'd make a man out of that son of mine.

GIRL FRIEND (*angry*): I don't want to be a member of your family. Half the time I don't want to be a member of *my own* family. And as for your son, he's just fine the way he is. But you have to let go of him.

MOTHER (*stunned*): I have to what?

GIRL FRIEND: You have to accept the fact that he's a grown man and let go.

MOTHER (*hurt and angry*): So who's holding on? Excuse me, darling. In Minsk where I come from, a person had respect for her family. You were grateful to be a member of a family.

GIRL FRIEND: These are not the dark ages of Minsk. You're living in a new era.

MOTHER: Honey, I have no degree, but I know a good recipe when I read the ingredients and this is some half-baked era.

GIRL FRIEND: I've got to run.

(*She gets up to leave.*)

MOTHER: People are always running from one thing to another. What I wouldn't give to be back in the "dark ages," as you put it.

GIRL FRIEND: Well, wishing for the past is a dangerous preoccupation.

MOTHER: Let me tell you, living in the present is no great shakes, either.

GIRL FRIEND: Well, it's been so good meeting with you.

(*She goes to shake her hand.*)

MOTHER: Likewise, I'm sure.

(*Mother takes her hand and pulls her close for a kiss on the cheek. Girl Friend tightens, then makes a speedy exit. Mother watches her exit with a grimace.*)

Oi, gottenu.*

(*She sits.*)

* Yiddish for "Oh, my God!"

VOICE OVER: "MICROWAVES"

Wife enters with a cup and saucer which she puts in front of Mother. She then sits down and begins to polish her nails. Mother takes a sip from cup, then spits it out.

MOTHER: This coffee tastes a little plasticky.

WIFE: It should taste great, it's from the new machine.

MOTHER: What machine?

WIFE: The Happy Coffee Machine. It makes it like fresh perked.

MOTHER: I don't understand how you young girls manage in these kitchens today.

WIFE: What, Mom?

MOTHER: All that machinery. You need a degree in engineering. Did I tell you about poor Helene's granddaughter? She lost half of her finger in one of those Cuisinart things that everyone's playing with. Cut it right to the bone.

WIFE: Stop.

MOTHER: And that microwave thing. You're going to give your family black lung disease or worse. I just know it.

WIFE (*losing patience*): But Mom, it's easy and it is safe. They've been tested by the government. I baked a ham in two minutes last night.

(*Mother winces.*)

And I can defrost and cook frozen vegetables in forty-five seconds. And I never have to scrub pans the way I used to.

MOTHER: When did you ever scrub pans? The pans have always gone into the dishwasher.

WIFE (*under her breath*): Oh, shut up.

MOTHER (*Mother hears her*): What did you say?

WIFE (*squirming*): Uh, I said . . . oh, so what.

(*Mother gives her a look.*)

Mom, you're always K-vetching!

MOTHER (*mocking her pronunciation*): K-vetching? About what am I kvetching?

WIFE: K-vetching about cooking.

MOTHER: Cooking is a dying art. People want to watch cooking, they turn on the television and watch Julia Child. There's nobody cooking in the kitchen. Oh, what's the difference? Everything we put in our mouths is going to give us cancer anyway. Pretty soon, all food is going to have to be stamped with a warning from the Surgeon General.

(*Enter Granddaughter.*)

GRANDDAUGHTER: Hi, Mommy.

WIFE: Hi, Cookie.

GRANDDAUGHTER: Hi, Grandma.

MOTHER: Hello, darling.

GRANDDAUGHTER: Guess what.

MOTHER: What sweetheart?

GRANDDAUGHTER: I got it.

MOTHER: What did you get, you cute little girl?

GRANDDAUGHTER: I got *it*.

WIFE (*with tears in her eyes*): You got *it?* Oh, baby . . .
(*Mother jumps up from her seat and gives her a slap on the face.*)

GRANDDAUGHTER (*pissed*): Grandma, what are you doing?

MOTHER: It's a tradition, sweetheart. When a little girl becomes a woman she gets a slap on the occasion.

(*Wife is livid about the slap and begins to deep breathe. Older Son enters.*)

OLDER SON (*oblivious*): Well, look who's here. Three generations of beautiful women.

(*They all wince. He notices wife is upset.*)

What's the matter?

WIFE: Your daughter just got it.

OLDER SON (*Rushing over to Granddaughter.*):

Cookie, you made the varsity cheerleading squad. Yea!

WIFE (*Moves over to Older Son.*):

No. No. She's *a woman.*

(*She exits offstage, crying.*)

MOTHER (*Over to Older Son.*):

It's for moments like this that I prayed for a daughter.

(*She exits offstage following Wife.*)

OLDER SON: What is going on here?

GRANDDAUGHTER: Daddy! (*embarrassed*) I got my period.

OLDER SON (*uncomfortable*): Well, that's nice. Isn't it? Oh . . .
well . . .

GRANDDAUGHTER: Yeah.

OLDER SON: Well, congratulations.

(*He tries to shake her hand, but she gives him a look.*)

I think I'll just celebrate with a little martini.

(*He moves toward hutch.*)

GRANDDAUGHTER: But Daddy, I heard Mom say you gave up
martinis.

OLDER SON (*Stops dead.*):

Oh yeah, well I guess I'll just see if there's any Gatorade in the
fridge!

(*They both exit.*)

VOICE OVER: "THE GIRL FRIEND SPEAKS"

GIRL FRIEND: Some people never get what they want. I generally get what I want, except when I get it, I realize, I don't want it anymore. Now every young woman is supposed to want to get married. Right? You accepted that as part of your destiny in life. So of course I got married and everyone was thrilled but me. Everyone was relieved but me. I became more anxious. I wanted to be single again. I got divorced—listen, any psychiatrist will tell you that it's against our nature to not have a partner. (*pause*) The fact of the matter is that what it all comes down to, what it really all comes down to, is mush.

(*Younger Son enters with sunglasses, a pocket mirror, and a razor blade. He sits at table.*)

You know, when you meet someone that really turns you on and your heart begins to pound and your stomach turns to mush. Unfortunately, mush never sustains itself. It fades away and the mind goes back to running the show again. I am experiencing a mild case of mush right now. But I'm so preoccupied with what's going to happen when the mush goes away that I'm not even enjoying the mush when it's here.

(*She exits.*)

VOICE OVER: "SELF REALIZATION"

Younger Son remains at table as Older Son runs onto the stage in a brand-new jogging outfit. He jogs and exercises as he speaks.

OLDER SON: Boy, that was a close one. Downing a pitcher of martinis a night. Mid-thirties crisis. Thank God I heard about jogging. I could be like that guy who suddenly clutched his heart while doing a summation speech before the jury. Now I jog instead of drink. Now I try to get it all out. Enough of this retentiveness. Enough. Life is too short. I am where I am. The past is prologue. That's what's engraved on the side of the Justice Department. I don't know, now I feel terrific. I can't stand being around unhappy people. They're so self-indulgent. Psychiatrists? Who the hell needs them? Two brisk miles around the neighborhood and the depression is gone. I'm going to live a long, long time. And what's more important (*he suddenly clutches his heart. A shooting pain which subsides momentarily. He laughs away the scare*) . . . I'm going to enjoy every minute of it.

(*He exits with a smile until a muscle in his back gives him another shooting pain.*)

VOICE OVER: "AN HONEST PERSON"

YOUNGER SON (*He chops cocaine on the mirror.*):

Well, you know I have nothing against jogging. I frankly don't choose to believe it does much more than give you torn ligaments and foot blisters, but if it makes you happy . . . no for me, it all has to do with perception. My perception of you, your perception of me, my perception of myself, your perception of yourself, and your perception of my perception of your perceptions. Look, I like drugs because I'm an honest person. You see, if I walk down the street and I see a bum curled up in a corner, or some rich person wearing an endangered animal for a coat, or people missing arms or legs or teeth or even hair—I don't look the other way—I don't give myself some rap about the horrors and the absurdities of urban life. No. I do what any other honest person would do—I get *really* depressed! (*He snorts a line.*) BUT, if I smoke a joint or pop a pill or snort something, my perception has been altered and reality has been sufficiently changed so that when I walk down the street, I'm lucky if I see anything at all.

(*He goes to snort another line. Blackout.*)

VOICE OVER: "SEVEN BEANS"

As the lights come up, Older Son, Wife, and Granddaughter are sitting at the table finishing their dessert. Grandson is staring into his dinner plate where seven lima beans remain.

GRANDDAUGHTER: Can I please be excused from the table?

WIFE: Finish telling us about school.

GRANDDAUGHTER: All right. In health class Miss Perceverse gave us a detailed lecture on pubic hair with these really gross slides of hair follicles and stuff that was really disgusting, and Jenny and I sat in the back laughing. Now can I please be excused from the table?

OLDER SON: Absolutely.

WIFE (*annoyed*): Help clear the table first.

(*Granddaughter begins clearing the table.*)

GRANDSON: Me too?

WIFE: Buddy, I told you that you are not leaving this table until you eat those vegetables. You remember the doctor's report?

GRANDSON: But the vegetables are overcooked.

OLDER SON: Buddy.

WIFE (*offended*): You cannot overcook vegetables in a microwave oven.

GRANDSON: Then the microwave oven needs a two-hundred-meal checkup.

(*Older Son chuckles.*)

WIFE: Don't be fresh.

GRANDSON: I'm not being fresh.

OLDER SON: Don't be fresh, Buddy. Just put the lima beans in your mouth and chew.

GRANDSON: Lima beans are disgusting. They squash in your mouth and they make me want to puke.

(*Granddaughter laughs. Wife snaps her finger and gives her an admonishing look. She exits with the dessert dishes.*)

WIFE: Buddy, are you going to force me to take disciplinary action? You know how much it hurts me to have to punish you.

GRANDSON: Everyone hates me.

WIFE: We don't hate you—we just hate your table manners and your eating habits.

(*She pushes the plate toward him. He turns away.*)

All right. All right.

(*She exits.*)

OLDER SON (*pleading and paternal, he goes over to Grandson*): Buddy, look, in this world of ours we can't always get to do what we want. We have to make compromises and sacrifices. Now look at Daddy. I loved smoking cigarettes and drinking martinis. But I realized that I had to make a change—a sacrifice.

GRANDSON: Daddy was a lush.

OLDER SON (*hurt*): Okay, Buddy, let's do Mommy a favor and eat one of those beans. Just swallow it. You don't have to chew it, just swallow it.

(*He holds Grandson's neck as he picks a bean up off the plate and puts it to his mouth. He tries gentle persuasion at first: "Come on Buddy, eat the bean." He gets carried away when Grandson won't budge and bends the kid's head back: "Do you want Daddy to smash this bean against your teeth? Open that mouth!" Wife enters and rushes over shocked at what appears to be her husband attacking their son. She grabs Older Son.*)

WIFE: Darling—I will take care of this.

(*Older Son suddenly realizes what he's been doing. He is shocked at his own behavior. He pats Grandson on the head and staggers to the door.*)

WIFE: Honey, you go lie down.

(*Older Son nods and exits, eating the bean.*)

WIFE: Now Buddy?

(*She pushes the plate toward him. He turns away.*)

Buddy, you know this hurts me more than it hurts you . . .

(*She takes a pair of handcuffs from her apron pocket and proceeds to shackle the child to the table.*)

. . . but you have got to learn to eat the food that is put in front of you like any normal child.

GRANDSON: There are no starving children in China. There was a revolution in China and everyone is doing just fine eating rice.

WIFE (*said with love and charm*): I never said anything about starving children in China, but in a very few minutes there may be a severely beaten child right here. Now look. There are only six little beans on your plate. Just think of all the nutrition and

lovely vitamins and minerals that are in those six beans—
AND YOU EAT THEM!

(*She exits.*)

GRANDSON (*to audience*): It's been a tough week. Being told
you're abnormal. Do you have any idea what that can do to a
vulnerable kid like me? Twelve pounds under and three inches
shy of the normal weight and height of a kid my age. I hate vegetables. Why can't I just take a little vitamin pill like all the kids
on TV? Does she seriously think five brussels sprouts or eighteen
green beans or six tablespoons of creamed spinach are going to
bring me up to average?

(*Shakes his head and looks back at handcuffs.*)

I could get out of this in a minute.

(*He pulls his hand out of the cuff.*)

It's not even such a good psychological ploy, but you know
what? She's right—it's gonna hurt her a hell of a lot more than it
hurts me.

(*Wife calls from offstage:* "How we doing in there?" *Grandson
takes beans from the plate and sticks them in his pocket. He then
puts his hand back in the handcuff and lowers his head.*)

WIFE (*Seeing a clean plate, she rushes over.*):

Now, that wasn't so terrible, was it, sweetie pie?

(*He shrugs a hesitant no and she takes off the handcuffs.*)

Guess what, cute little boy?

(*He rubs his wrist as if he were hurt by the cuffs.*)

There's some junket pudding and some Ready Whip in the
fridge for your dessert.

(*She leans over to touch him.*)

Okay?

(*He leans away.*)

GRANDSON: Mom, I don't feel so good.

WIFE: What?

GRANDSON: I feel kind of sick. Oh, God, Mom, I think I'm going to puke.

(*He dashes from the room.*)

WIFE (*following*): Buddy!

VOICE OVER: "TELL ME ANYTHING"

Younger Son rushes into the space with Girl Friend yakking behind.

GIRL FRIEND (exasperated): Look, I'm just trying to get things out in the open. I'm a little bit older than you. I've been married—things are different for me—I'm working on opening up—talking things out.

YOUNGER SON: So talk things out—

GIRL FRIEND: I don't love you.

YOUNGER SON: Fine.

GIRL FRIEND: I mean I do love you, but I'm not in love with you . . .

YOUNGER SON: Fine.

GIRL FRIEND: Which makes it difficult for me to see you.

YOUNGER SON: Why does that make it difficult?

GIRL FRIEND: Difficult because I am a person who really needs to be in love.

YOUNGER SON: Yeah, so?

GIRL FRIEND: So, you're not really the kind of person I want to be in love with . . .

YOUNGER SON: Oh?

GIRL FRIEND: . . . besides which, you really don't want me falling in love with you.

YOUNGER SON: I don't?

GIRL FRIEND: Take it from me, you hardly know me. The minute I declare my love for someone, I feel compelled to be unfaithful.

YOUNGER SON: Me, too.

GIRL FRIEND: There, you see, I could never have a relationship with someone who was unfaithful to me.

YOUNGER SON: That makes no sense, but I think I understand perfectly. (*lovingly*) Look, if you want to cheat on me, you can.

GIRL FRIEND: That's just what I mean—you're so goddammed wishy-washy. Can't you take a stand? I hate being able to walk all over you. It's just not going to work.

YOUNGER SON: Okay, okay. Relax.

GIRL FRIEND: Besides which, I have a confession to make that's very embarrassing and is really going to turn you off.

YOUNGER SON: Try me.

GIRL FRIEND: I have crabs.

(*Younger Son stops dead.*)

I picked them up at the clinic somehow.

YOUNGER SON (*at a loss for words*): . . . that's too bad.

GIRL FRIEND: That's too bad? That's all you can say? Don't you ever express anger?

YOUNGER SON: What is it with you anyway?

GIRL FRIEND: I think it's important that we be able to tell each other everything—without being uptight.

YOUNGER SON: Tell me anything. I'm not uptight.

GIRL FRIEND: What if I tell you I've slept with women?

YOUNGER SON: Women?

GIRL FRIEND: That's what I said.

YOUNGER SON: That doesn't threaten me.

GIRL FRIEND: Any psychiatrist will tell you that it's a natural urge to be attracted to your own sex. But if the idea of that bothers you, you certainly can tell me.

YOUNGER SON: I used to have this thing for little girls.

GIRL FRIEND: What kind of thing?

YOUNGER SON: You know . . .

GIRL FRIEND: Little women you mean?

YOUNGER SON: Girls.

GIRL FRIEND: Girls?

YOUNGER SON: Girls.

GIRL FRIEND (*disgusted*): Girls. (*big breath*) Well, anything goes, right? We live in the unshockable age. Words have no meaning. Everybody's done everything.

YOUNGER SON: Right. We're free! And we're oh so contemporary. Liberation is the name of the day.

GIRL FRIEND: Do you have any idea what Freud says about doing "things" with little girls?

YOUNGER SON: Fuck Freud.

GIRL FRIEND (*angry again*): Shut up.

YOUNGER SON: You suck your thumb. What do your psychiatrists say about that?

GIRL FRIEND (*hurt*): I do not!

YOUNGER SON: You do too. At night when you go to bed.

(*He makes thumb-sucking motion.*)

GIRL FRIEND: That's an unforgivable accusation!

YOUNGER SON (*pulling back*): I think it's kind of cute.

GIRL FRIEND: It's retentive, that's what it is—but no more so than you, hiding under that hideous hat of yours with a joint stuck in your mouth like some maternal nipple substitute!

YOUNGER SON (*flies off the handle*): All right. You won. Look, I'm angry.

(*He slams his hand against the wall or the table.*)

Let's call the whole thing off.

GIRL FRIEND (*a moment of silence*): Well, I feel sort of better now that everything's out in the open. Communication is very important.

YOUNGER SON: So's mental health. I shudder to think what you do to your patients.

GIRL FRIEND: If they can survive me, you *know* they're ready for the real world.

(*Silence.*)

Let's just be friends, huh? Let's not succumb to the predisposed notions of conventional relationships. What do you say?

(*He shrugs.*)

You're awfully cute, you know that?

(*He shrugs again. She goes over to him and gives him a kiss.*)

YOUNGER SON (*He walks away.*):

Under this new unconventional disposition, do friends get to make . . . whoopee?

GIRL FRIEND: I don't see why not.

(*Girl Friend exits past Younger Son who holds open the door. Younger Son is about to follow, when he stops and shrugs his shoulders and smiles to the audience. He then exits.*)

VOICE OVER: "A MOTHER'S HEART"

Older Son and Mother enter together. Mother is wearing a bathrobe. Older Son is carrying a large box for the Mother.

MOTHER: Honey, you're so good to help your mother out.

OLDER SON: Where do you want this?

MOTHER: In the closet, darling.

(*He moves to the closet, she goes to the hutch and gets a piece of cake.*)

Then come have a delicious piece of cake.

OLDER SON: I just ate.

(*He drops box in doorway.*)

What was in there anyway?

MOTHER: Dishes.

OLDER SON (*He goes to the table and sits.*):

Helen is giving you dishes? You've got enough dishes to serve all of Grossinger's.

MOTHER: She couldn't take them all to Florida.

(*At some point she puts the cake before him on the table.*)

OLDER SON: So why didn't she throw them out?

MOTHER: Throw them out! Those plates mean a lot to her. Oh, excuse me. You paper-plate people would never understand.

Remember those books you've shlepped everywhere? You never look at those books—it's the same thing. You don't like the cake?

OLDER SON: I just ate, I'm not hungry.

MOTHER (*She laughs and leans over taking a piece of the cake on the fork and lifting it toward his mouth.*):
Try a little piece.

OLDER SON: (*He protests, "No. Please no," accidentally bumping the fork and seeing the cake fall to the floor. He angrily grabs the fork.*)
Okay, I'll eat the cake!

MOTHER (*She kisses him.*):
You always had a beautiful appetite when you lived here, you and your brother both.
(*She sits down.*)
So have you heard from him lately?

OLDER SON: Un ugh.

MOTHER: Me neither.

OLDER SON: It's the carnivore.

MOTHER: What's the what?

OLDER SON: His girl friend.

MOTHER (*enthused*): You don't like her?
(*He shrugs.*)

OLDER SON: Do you?

MOTHER (*she thinks for a moment choosing her words carefully*): She's not a malicious person, am I right?

(*He eats.*)

Oi, I hardly ever see him. Between that good for nothing job of his, and now this carnivore person—and Helen's going to Florida —who have I got?

OLDER SON (*carefully*): Listen, Mom, you know Florida is not the worst place for a person to live.

MOTHER (*indignant*): You want to get rid of me?

OLDER SON: I didn't say that.

MOTHER: You'd love for me to leave.

OLDER SON: Mom—

MOTHER: I know what you're thinking.

OLDER SON (*angry*): How do you know what I'm thinking?

MOTHER: Because a mother's heart knows.

OLDER SON (*fed up*): Will you stop it with the mother's heart stuff. You talk to me like I'm still a child.

MOTHER: You and your brother act like children, so what do you expect? (*injured*) Oh well, I've got no one—who cares, I'm just yesterday's dishes.

(*She gets up from the table.*)

OLDER SON: Will you stop it.

MOTHER (*looking at the half-eaten cake*): You didn't like the cake.

OLDER SON (*defeated*): I loved the cake, I loved the cake, I'm just not hungry.

(*Mother clears the table. She comes downstage plate in hand to address the audience.*)

MOTHER: What does he know? For all he thinks, a woman my age is supposed to enjoy being alone. You know something? I'm hungry, and let me tell you it's not for food. Oi what I wouldn't give for a little hanky-panky. Oh, don't get me wrong—nothing major. Just a kiss, a hug now and then, a tender touch on the back of the neck. Something to make you feel like a woman—but there's not a man around, and believe me I've looked. And Clark Gable I'm not seeking, either. Listen, I'm not the type to put on false eyelashes, get myself all dolled-up, and go off hotsie-totsie to Miami. (*tearful*) Helen's going to hate it, I just know. (*sigh*) In Minsk in such an event, you married your husband's brother. In Minsk, you had a family that stood firm at your side giving you love and support. This one, he'll never understand.

(*Lights come up as if nothing has passed and she moves back upstage.*)

MOTHER: So, what are you doing for Mother's Day?

OLDER SON (*laughs at the absurdity of it all*): Did you know that there are more suicides on Mother's Day than any other holiday?

MOTHER: Well, with what you have to put up with, I'm not surprised.

(*She puts plate away.*)

OLDER SON: It's not the mothers who are killing themselves.

MOTHER: Another joker.

OLDER SON: I'll tell you what. I'll take everybody out for dinner.

MOTHER: You will? But not to one of those fast-food establishments like last year.

OLDER SON: That was not a "fast-food" establishment. That was a very expensive smorgasbord restaurant.

MOTHER: You know what, sweetheart, why doesn't everybody come here for dinner?

OLDER SON: No, no, no. I'm taking everyone out.

MOTHER: Don't forget to invite your brother.

OLDER SON: For you, Mom, I'll even invite the carnivore.

(*Mother exits. There is the sound of a horn or the quack of a duck and a telegram drops from above. It is in the mouth of a dead chicken à la "You Bet Your Life." Older Son, taken off guard, cautiously approaches it and takes it down. The chicken disappears above. He reads aloud with a certain irony.*)

OLDER SON: Your wife, daughter, and son and mother were just killed by a plane that accidentally crashed into your house. Stop. You are entitled to $100,000 in life and accident insurance and selling your property will bring you an additional $124,000. Stop. This is it, buddy. You're free at last. Everyone loves you more now that destiny has struck such a painful blow. Stop. Go ahead, parade around in women's clothes. (*nervous*) Stop. Go ahead, run away. Go as long as you want. Act like a maniac. You are finally alone again. Isn't that what you've always . . . wanted? Stop!

(*He exits.*)

VOICE OVER: "THINKING OUT LOUD"

Granddaughter enters in a cloud of cigarette smoke. She is wearing a seductive prom dress, and enters carrying her high heels and a lit cigarette. She walks with great sophistication and speaks as if she is thirty-four and not fourteen.

GRANDDAUGHTER: Stephen Franklin and I will probably get married our second year of college, and I'll have decided that I really don't want to be a dermatologist; after all he'll become the rich doctor. We'll find a big house in the country and I'll fix it up real cute and we'll have a shaggy dog and two kids. One boy and one girl. Jenny and Stephen junior. And I'll be the best mother in town. My kids can do pretty much whatever they want, as long as I don't have to know about it. Of course, they'll have a curfew and if they don't obey me, (*mean*) then I'll really give it to them. But we'll all be such good friends. During the days I'll lunch at that cute little restaurant across the street from Bloomingdale's, and then I'll cross the street buying the best of silks and satins, and I'll even buy diamonds and rubies at Tiffany's, of course.

(*She sits on the table and puts on her shoes.*)

And the kids will grow up to be real cute and successful and they'll get married and then Stephen and I will take that cruise to Tahiti we've always talked about. And he'll joke to me about the time he tried to pull off my blouse on the bus, and we'll both laugh (*returning to the bitchy teenager*) hah—I don't think I'll ever forgive him for that! (*back to being sophisticated*) But, Stephen will probably die because he worked real hard and was under so much pressure—and then I'll be single again. (*She laughs, then gets embarrassed.*) Oh, I'll be real depressed for a while. But then I'll probably meet a new mate, and who knows what will happen?

VOICE OVER: "TAHITIAN PARADISE"

GRANDSON: Lauren Bacall, I would suggest putting out your cigarette as Mommy and Daddy have just pulled up in the driveway.

(*He makes a mad dash to get rid of the cigarette. She gets off the table. Her balance on high heels is tenuous at best.*)

GRANDDAUGHTER: Quick!

(*Wife and Older Son enter. Older Son is carrying a bucket of fried chicken.*)

WIFE: Oh my God, you're dressed already. Darling, you look just lovely.

OLDER SON: Holy smokes—you're a knockout!

(*Granddaughter begins to walk very slowly and very cautiously.*)

GRANDSON: You better be careful in those heels.

WIFE/OLDER SON/GRANDDAUGHTER: QUIET.

OLDER SON: Where did you get that dress?

WIFE: It was my prom dress.

OLDER SON: I thought you were supposed to do that with bridal gowns?

GRANDSON: She's nominated to be in the Queen's Court. It's the same thing.

WIFE: Oh, honey, maybe you'll be "Queen of an Evening in Tahitian Paradise."

OLDER SON: What?

GRANDSON: An Evening in Tahitian Paradise. That's what they call their prom.

(*Older Son and Wife stand on either side of Granddaughter.*)

OLDER SON: Oh. (*as an aside to Wife*) Honey, isn't that dress awfully low cut?

GRANDDAUGHTER: Daddy, all the girls are wearing plunging necklines this season.

WIFE: Honey, have you got that little purse?

(*She nods yes.*)

OLDER SON: Listen, princess. If this Franklin character gives you a hard time, just call and we'll come and get you immediately.

GRANDDAUGHTER: Oh Daddy, he's matured.

WIFE: Sweetheart, do you have a hankie?

(*She nods yes.*)

OLDER SON: Now, who's driving you?

GRANDDAUGHTER: Franklin's older brother.

WIFE: And you have that new lip gloss I got you?

GRANDDAUGHTER: Uh huh.

OLDER SON: Well, I want you home by midnight.

GRANDDAUGHTER (*exploding*): Midnight, that's ridiculous! Everyone is going to be at the party until at least one o'clock.

OLDER SON (*to Wife*): Wait a minute. She's not even fourteen yet. Right?

GRANDSON: She's fourteen.

OLDER SON: Right.

WIFE: One o'clock.

OLDER SON: Twelve fifteen.

GRANDSON: Do I hear twelve forty-five?

TOGETHER: QUIET.

WIFE: Go get the camera.
(*Grandson exits.*)
One o'clock. Darling, times have changed.

OLDER SON: I want her covered. She's not leaving this house until she's covered.

WIFE (*shaking her head in disbelief at Granddaughter*): Honey, I have a little surprise for you.
(*She exits.*)

OLDER SON: Pumpkin, come over here. I want to talk to you.
(*Granddaughter stumbles downstage to the Older Son.*)
First of all, Cookie, I want you to know that if I find out you've been drinking or smoking marijuana, you will be grounded for months and months and your allowance will be withheld until you go to college.

GRANDDAUGHTER (*annoyed*): Yes, Dad.

OLDER SON: Now, Mommy has told you about boys, hasn't she?

GRANDDAUGHTER (*innocent*): No, Dad. What about boys?

OLDER SON: You know.

GRANDDAUGHTER (*not giving him a break*): No, I don't have the slightest idea.

OLDER SON: Cookie, in that dress you better have some idea. Now come on. Boys and girls—let me put it like this. (*angry*) If there's one mark on that neck of yours, I'm going to pull that kid's lips off with my bare hands.

(*Wife enters unnoticed with a pair of earrings.*)

GRANDDAUGHTER (*pissed*): Don't worry, I don't screw around!

WIFE (*stunned*): Cookie!! (*to Older Son*) Sweetheart, this prom is chaperoned by their teachers.

OLDER SON: That's what worries me.

WIFE: Look, honey, my favorite.

(*Puts earrings on her.*)

You look so grown-up, I just can't believe my eyes.

(*Gives her a hug.*)

Oh, I'm so filled with emotion. (*crying*) Where's the camera?!

(*Grandson flying in from offstage.*)

GRANDSON: I've got it. Now everybody over here.

(*Grandson directs them with great fuss to stand around the Granddaughter.*)

Smile, everyone smile. Pull the dress out Cookie. Everybody say sex.

ALL: Sex!

(*Grandson takes the flash picture. Wife and Older Son fume at the realization of what they just said. Grandson and Granddaughter laugh as lights fade to black.*)

VOICE OVER: "SMALL SPACES"

From some unsuspecting place in the set.

YOUNGER SON: I don't know what it is with me and small spaces. I feel like I'm in a coffin or something. And rooms today are getting so small. Smaller and smaller. Pretty ridiculous, huh? I mean if I told that to anyone they would think something was really the matter. But you know, after a while, neurosis is such a bore.

(Coming into the space and setting it up for the restaurant as he speaks.)

I don't know. There have been times when I've felt like there was this big door slamming right behind me—the air supply slowly being exhausted—the ceiling imperceptively coming down on top of me. Just as the walls are about to touch my skin, I shout for help, but when I open my mouth, nothing comes out. You think there's no one there to hear you, but one day you understand: they just can't find you. You've simply taken yourself too far away. Become too distant. Too hidden. Someplace deep inside—very dark and very, very small.

(He lights a candle on the table and the room is returned to the identical appearance of the beginning of the play, except the table now seats five.)

VOICE OVER: "DESSERT"

*The Mother, Older Son, Wife, Grandson, and Granddaughter
enter. They sit and stare at each other for a moment. Younger
Son gives each a menu. When he gets to the Older Son, he delib-
erately drops his menu on the floor.*

OLDER SON: How was your day?

(There is a general moan in response.)

YOUNGER SON: Would anyone care for a drink?

(Older Son starts to order, Wife stops him.)

Our specials tonight are roast sirloin topped with our special
Béarnaise sauce; chicken marengo, a delicious casserole which
we age ourselves; braised sweetbreads, the best of organ meats—

OLDER SON: I'm dying for a cigarette and a drink.

WIFE: Darling, you've been so good up till now.

MOTHER: This food doesn't appeal to me at all. We should have
stayed at my house and ate.

YOUNGER SON: We have a wonderful Brunswick stew, a corn
bread tamale pie, and a shad roe soufflé. And of course I can
offer you crabs.

WIFE: I would like the chicken à la king, please.

YOUNGER SON: No. You don't really want the chicken à la king.

WIFE: I don't.

YOUNGER SON: It's not up to par.

OLDER SON: How's the fresh blue fish?

YOUNGER SON: Frozen.

GRANDDAUGHTER: I'll have the spaghetti platter.

YOUNGER SON: I'm sorry, we're out of spaghetti.

WIFE: How can you be out of spaghetti?

YOUNGER SON: You find roaches in the spaghetti box.

GRANDSON: I'll take a hamburger, french fries, and a Coke.

YOUNGER SON: I'm sorry, we only serve hamburgers at lunch.

MOTHER (*hostile*): I'll have this filet of sole special, as long as you approve, of course.

YOUNGER SON: An excellent choice, madame. That has a lovely stuffing made of crabmeat, shrimp, and bacon. Would you like some fried pork rinds with that?

MOTHER (*gagging*): I don't want it. (*gives Older Son a pained look*) I told you.

OLDER SON: If you had your way, we'd be eating at your house every night!

MOTHER: So?

OLDER SON: I'll have a double martini up, two olives. You can get it now, while we reconsider the menu, sir.

WIFE: Sweetheart. A doubled martini?

YOUNGER SON (*as he writes the order down*): He's a big boy—let him have a martini if he wants.

OLDER SON: Mind your own business or we'll stop pretending we don't know you.

YOUNGER SON: You don't know me.

OLDER SON (*the anger is about to burst*): Forget it—and don't expect a tip from me. Where's the cigarette machine?

YOUNGER SON: You don't have to go to the cigarette machine—Cookie will give you a cigarette.

MOTHER AND WIFE: What?!

GRANDDAUGHTER: Shut up, Uncle Sonny.

YOUNGER SON: It's okay, Cookie—give him one. In fact I wouldn't mind one myself.

(*She hesitates.*)

Well, come on, Cookie, come on!

(*Granddaughter pulls out a pack of cigarettes and begins passing them out.*)

GRANDSON: I want one, too.

WIFE: Buddy!

YOUNGER SON: You want to stunt your growth and be a freak?

(*Grandson jumps up from the table.*)

GRANDSON: You're the freak.

(*The table explodes as everyone begins fighting with each other. Grandson goes under table, and Older Son shouts.*)

OLDER SON: Where are you going?

GRANDSON: I dropped my napkin.

YOUNGER SON: He's going to hide.

WIFE: That's not normal.

YOUNGER SON (*loud*): That's right—we're all abnormal.

MOTHER (*staring out at the audience in a state of shock*): Sonny, hush up. Everybody's looking at us. Behave yourself.
(*They realize they've been discovered.*)

WIFE: My goodness, can't we have one meal in peace?

OLDER SON: Are you going to get me a double martini or am I going to have to get up and pour the goddam thing myself?

YOUNGER SON: We're out of olives.

OLDER SON: You're not out of olives—you're out of your mind—you've finally cracked up.

YOUNGER SON: I'm not out of my mind—I'm just trying to open up—to provoke a little family dialogue.

MOTHER: Now boys, let's not fight—please, not in public.

YOUNGER SON: Mom, he's always picking on me.

OLDER SON: I'm not picking on you.
(*They all begin to argue and fight again. They all lose control.*)

MOTHER (*slamming fists on the table*): QUIET!
(*They pull themselves together.*)

OLDER SON: Where's the cigarette machine?

(*Younger Son points offstage indifferently.*)

GRANDDAUGHTER: Don't you like my brand?

OLDER SON (*seething*): You're going to get it when we get home.
(*He exits.*)

WIFE: I just can't believe my eyes and ears. Excuse me, dear,
charming, loving, and ever-considerate brother-in-law, where's
the ladies room?
(*He helps her out of her seat and points offstage.*)
Now, I'm going to go powder my nose—

YOUNGER SON: You mean you're going to take a leak.
(*Granddaughter cracks up. Wife exits tearfully.*)

MOTHER (*standing up and grabbing him*):
Sonny, I want you to be nice—please—I don't know what's gotten into you.

GRANDDAUGHTER (*Begins to exit also.*):
He's high as a kite, Grandma.

MOTHER: Cookie, where are you going?

GRANDDAUGHTER: I'm going to call Stephen Franklin. (*in her sophisticated voice*) He understands me!
(*She exits.*)

MOTHER (*at a loss*): Sweetheart—Sonny, are you taking a trip?

YOUNGER SON: No, Mom—I'm not stoned. I'm just trying to let it
all hang out—I'm trying to open myself up to the world. Let
every thought be exposed to the whole family.

MOTHER (*to the audience*): Do you know what he's talking about?

(*Girl Friend enters.*)

GIRL FRIEND: He's beginning to connect with his feelings (*Mother mutters an "oi"*) but he's afraid to reach out and accept the people that are familiar to him. (*embracing Younger Son*) Come with me to a safe and small room where you can feel free and unafraid.

(*The Girl Friend gives him a passionate kiss in front of the Mother, then they exit in the embrace. She sits alone at the table.*)

MOTHER: Oi, I've tried. Well, a person does all they can, right? So now they've all run off. It's the age, thank God it's not mine. Still, a mother worries. They'll run and they'll run and you know what? They'll end up right back where they started. Oi, if they had just one cold day in Minsk, believe me they wouldn't run so hard. No one understands me and no one even tries!

(*Younger Son enters unnoticed.*)

I got a letter from Helen in Florida yesterday—

YOUNGER SON (*From across the room, he startles the Mother.*):

Hey, Ninotchka.

(*She turns to him.*)

We have decided to all go over to your house for flanken . . . but *only* if you stop talking about Minsk!

MOTHER (*indignant*): Forever?

YOUNGER SON (*with a smile*): For now.

MOTHER (*nodding her head yes*): Oi, for now.

(*Younger Son exits. Mother prepares to leave the table. She blows out the candle.*)

MOTHER: You know what Helen got in Florida? (*with sweet revenge*) Hanky panky!

(*Blackout.*)

V

\

DATE DUE			